MINISTERING
TO
ALCOHOLICS

by

John E. Keller

AUGSBURG Publishing House • Minneapolis

MINISTERING TO ALCOHOLICS

Copyright © 1966 Augsburg Publishing House

Library of Congress Catalog Card No. 66-22560

International Standard Book No. 0-8066-0618-5

MANUFACTURED IN THE UNITED STATES OF AMERICA

FOREWORD

In 1955, upon request of the Board of Directors of what is now Lutheran Social Service of Minnesota, the Executive Committee of the American Lutheran Church extended me a call to serve as chaplain with the special assignment of learning about alcoholism and counseling with alcoholics.

At that time, Dr. Luthard Gjerde, Executive Director of Lutheran Social Service, and Dr. Fredric Norstad, who was then Director of Chaplaincy Services of the agency, were the two men who initially recognized the need for this kind of ministry.

Their awareness of the need for greater understanding and concern within the church was sharpened through their close relationship with Dr. Nelson Bradley, Superintendent of the Willmar State Hospital, Willmar, Minn. He had developed an outstanding state treatment program for alcoholics within the hospital, and was vitally interested in the spiritual aspects of the problem of alcoholism. Dr. Bradley encouraged them in their desire to call a chaplain to serve in the Alcoholism Treatment Section. So it was that a special ministry to alcoholics came into being. Through this ministry it was felt that the church's understanding and concern would be enlarged and its ministry to alcoholics and their families would become more effective.

Dr. Bradley, with other members of his staff, Dr. Jean Rossi, Dr. Daniel Anderson, and the A.A. counselors, contributed greatly to the understanding necessary for the development of this kind of ministry.

iii

However, I am singling out Fred E., one of the counselors. To know him and to be able to share in his knowledge has been most meaningful and of inestimable value. I came to feel that he unknowingly is one of God's special kind of people. So it is to him that I dedicate this book.

Presently this ministry is carried on under the Lutheran Institute of Human Ecology at the Rehabilitation Center, Lutheran General Hospital, Park Ridge, Illinois. The Center was dedicated on March 7, 1969, for treatment, education, training, and research in alcoholism.

Acknowledgment is given also to Mrs. Marilyn Boe, Mrs. Mary Goodwin, and Mrs. Karen Kowert, secretaries who did the typing as the manuscript evolved, to Mrs. Solvig Nesset, who did the initial editing before the manuscript was sent to the publisher, and to Mrs. Betty Stadler, who did the typing of the revisions for the third printing.

JOHN E. KELLER

TABLE OF CONTENTS

INTRODUCTION

The parish pastor is frequently approached for help with the problem of alcoholism. Because of certain popular misconceptions, he may hesitate to become involved. We are still living with the invalid ideas, for instance, that only an alcoholic can help an alcoholic, that alcoholics avoid clergymen, that clergymen really shouldn't work with alcoholics, that alcoholics cannot be helped until they are ready to quit drinking. Further, alcoholism is often only thought of as being fantastically complex, and alcoholics are often pictured as being very difficult, if not impossible, to help. Alcoholism is a complex illness, but it is also true that alcoholics are human beings with an illness about which much is understood and from which many may recover.

Although a great deal remains to be learned about this illness, a great deal *is* known, and the pastor who is acquainted with the present body of knowledge can enrich his ministry to and effectiveness with alcoholics and their families. Certainly the pastor needs to become aware of when and to whom he should make referrals, but he also needs to recognize that there is much that he can do as a counselor. In fact, in many communities he may be the primary source of help at a given point in the helping process. It is important, therefore, that he not "sell himself short." Rather, he should become involved, enlarge his understanding of and communicate his concern for the alcoholic.

Although we have been talking about "alcoholism" for years, there is growing agreement today that there are "alcoholisms."[1] Here,

---

[1] E. M. Jellinek, *The Disease Concept of Alcoholism*, College and University Press, New Haven, Conn., in association with Hillhouse Press, New Brunswick, N.J., pp. 36-41.

vii

however, we will be talking about the alcoholism described by Jellinek as "gamma alcoholism," which is most typical in our culture, and which is described in the 44 Progressive Symptoms developed by Dr. E. M. Jellinek, with the phenomena of loss of control, downward progression, and addiction.

Describing alcoholism in these terms (in this specific context), we see it as an illness from which there can be no recovery without outside help. We consider as atypical the person who, in his drinking, seemed to fit this description and then recovered on his own in the sense that he quit drinking and did not harbor resentment or self-pity. There is the possibility that either this person was not an alcoholic according to the above description even though it appeared so, or that outside help, even though such help was not apparent, brought about the acceptance of powerlessness and the self-honesty which are essential in recovery.

It should also be noted that all of Dr. Harry Tiebout's articles, from which extensive quotes have been used, are available from the National Council on Alcoholism, 2 East 103rd Street, New York, N.Y. 10029. The pastor is urged to write for and carefully study all of the reprints.

J.E.K.

I.

UNDERSTANDING ALCOHOLISM
AND
ACCEPTING ALCOHOLICS

When Alcoholics Anonymous came into existence in the mid-1930's, light began to shine into the darkness that surrounded alcoholism. Through the spiritual program of this fellowship, alcoholics began to recover. The alcoholic in A.A. was sober no matter what medicine, psychiatry, or the church thought about his drinking problem and what he needed for sobriety. It is only natural, therefore, as we seek to enlarge our understanding of alcoholism and alcoholics, that we look to the program of Alcoholics Anonymous.

Understanding from A.A.

Strangely enough, we discover that A.A. tells us just what the church has been saying for years. The alcoholic is powerless over alcohol, and his hope is ultimately in God. But A.A. recognizes that, while the alcoholic surely needs God, he just as surely does not need moralism. Deep within most alcoholics there is already enough moralism to make them feel that there is no hope, even in God. With this very basic insight into these feelings of the alcoholic, A.A. provides the kind of understanding and acceptance that he needs. As a part of this fellowship he comes to realize that there *is* hope, gains the courage to take an honest look at his alcoholism, and assumes personal responsibility for his problem.

Another important aspect of the fellowship is the emphasis on self-honesty as an absolute essential. One who has had an oppor-

God ≠ moralism we often think so

1

tunity to witness and be a part of this experience in their small group meetings and with alcoholics on an individual basis feels keenly its meaning and value. In fact, he is left with the wish that there could be more of this within the Christian fellowship. Honest mutual sharing for mutual strengthening is an enriching, revitalizing experience.

In A.A. the alcoholic is confronted with a spiritual way of life— the Twelve Steps of recovery. The individual and corporate lives of the group serve as living epistles of the program's effectiveness. The alcoholic is not told that God will remove his problem. Rather, recovering alcoholics tell him that they have come to believe that God gives the alcoholic strength to stay sober one day at a time. After surrendering to his powerlessness and committing his life to the care of God, as he understands him, each day, the alcoholic takes a searching and fearless moral inventory of himself. This is followed by admitting to God, to himself, and to another human being, the exact nature of his wrongs. Interestingly enough, A.A. says that here the real spiritual experience begins.

Having made such an admission, the alcoholic becomes ready to have God remove his defects and humbly asks God to remove them. He makes a list of people he has harmed, becomes willing to make amends to them all, makes amends directly whenever possible, except when to do so would injure himself or others, and continues to take a daily inventory, promptly admitting any wrongdoing. Further, he seeks through prayer and meditation to improve his conscious contact with God, praying only for knowledge of his will and for power to carry out that will. Finally, having had a spiritual awakening as a result of these steps, he seeks to carry this message to other alcoholics and to practice these principles in all his affairs. (Another section will deal in detail with A.A. and the Twelve Steps.)

Inherent in the recovery program offered in the Twelve Steps is a fact of great significance to the understanding of alcoholism. The fact which first confronts the alcoholic in the Twelve Steps is the reality of his drinking. Because the drinking is compulsive and because the mark of alcoholism is powerlessness over alcohol, the drinking is recognized as the *immediate* problem even though it may not be the basic problem. The *immediate reason* for the drinking is loss of control. This powerlessness is not simply the inability to predict what will happen after the first drink—to control the amount consumed. It is also the inability to eventually not take the first drink. Many alcoholics say that they can "take it or leave it"—but they always eventually take it if they try under their own power not to drink. An alcoholic put it this way: "I don't know when I'm going to start, and when I start I don't know when I'm going to stop." This is total loss of control, and this loss is permanent. It will always be with the alcoholic no matter how many years he has lived without a drink. On the basis of present knowledge, the hope for controlled drinking is to be discarded.

And so the drinking, which was at first a symptom, is no longer merely a symptom. The symptom itself has become an illness—an addiction—that requires direct treatment.[1] To ignore this fact and concentrate on resolving the underlying emotional conflicts "resembles searching for causes of a fire while the blaze itself goes unchecked."[2] We in the church must remember this. As long as the alcoholic is unaware of the reality of his powerlessness or is protecting himself from this truth by rationalization and alibi, it is often impossible to help him in regard to any underlying problems for which he may also need help. He is neither ready to be nor capable of being honest with himself.

Understanding from Theology

We can further enlarge our understanding by becoming acquainted with what medicine, psychiatry, psychology, sociology, and other allied professions can teach us about alcoholism. However, at the

---

[1]Harry S. Tiebout, "Direct Treatment of a Symptom," reprint from *Problems of Addiction and Habituation*, Greene and Stratton, Inc.

[2]Margaret B. Bailey and Estelle Fuchs, "Alcoholism and the Social Worker," *Social Work*, Journal of the National Association of Social Workers, Vol. 5, No. 4, October 1960, pp. 18-19.

same time we need to try to understand the problem within the framework of our faith regarding God and man.

Basic to the Christian faith is the belief that in Holy Scriptures and in his Son Jesus Christ, God has revealed himself as Person. He is *the* Person who had as his basic purpose in creation the creating of persons. He, the Person, created man, the person. This is the meaning of "created man in his own image." God created man so that there might be life in and with relationship. Only persons can live in relationship.

He created persons so that we might live in perfect loving and trusting relationship with him as the Person. This was to be the ultimate relationship of life. Thus, the first commandment is, "You shall love the Lord your God with all your heart and soul and strength and mind."

But he also created us to live in perfect loving relationship with ourselves as persons and with other persons. The second great commandment is, "You shall love your neighbor as yourself."

Put another way, man was created to be fully human in his relationship with God, with himself, and with others.

Man became estranged in the totality of these relationships for which he was created. No longer did he have either the desire or the capacity to just be the created one—to be fully human in his relationships with God, self, and other persons. Man's problem isn't that he is too human, but that he cannot be fully human. Man is incapable of being the person he was created to be and ought to be. The only *true* person and *true* human man has seen live on earth is Jesus Christ, true God and true man.

Man now, by nature, is incapable of letting God be God. He is unable and unwilling to be the created person, the truly dependent person, in relationship to the Creator Person—unable and unwilling to love, trust, and obey God above everyone and everything. Egocentric, hostile, and defiant towards God, the created person perceives himself as the Omnipotent One—the Person.

In this condition man perceives himself at the center of life and feels that people and all of life ought to be just the way *he thinks* they ought to be, particularly in relationship to himself. Together with this, he will not let himself really become aware of and fully accept his own imperfections. This reality will frequently be disguised by *apparent* feelings of imperfection while he harbors the deep inner feeling that if there is imperfection within him, *he* ought to be able to overcome his imperfection and become perfect. He is in the contradiction of trying to avoid his imperfection by denial or by blaming others for it, and yet living with the feeling that being imperfect, *he*—if only *he*, but surely *he*—ought to be able to be perfect. And this is not only the need to be a perfect human, which no one can be, but in actuality the need to be God himself.

This is man's condition—bondage to himself as *the* person in his estrangement from the Person who is God.

But God remains God, and his intentions for man stand. Man remains a person created by God for a relationship of loving God with all his heart and soul and strength and mind. Sensing this and recognizing that he is unable to be as he was created to be and ought to be, man feels guilty before God. Just as Adam and Eve sought to hide from God, man, consciously or unconsciously, seeks to escape God or gain his favor to resolve his feelings of guilt. By nature man does not and cannot believe that God *really* loves him *as he is.*

Saint Augustine has said that man's soul will be restless until it rests again in God. The anxiety of estrangement in this ultimate relationship in life may not be man's most conscious anxiety. But theologically it is man's most basic anxiety.

To the restless, anxious, estranged person there comes the good news—the Gospel. God has taken on human flesh in the person of his Son Jesus Christ. In Christ, God comes among us and shows us that he really does love us and wants us now and forever, that he is for us, not against us, that we need to be and have been reconciled unto him, that the estrangement has been overcome, that we are his redeemed, justified, forgiven children. All that was needed to accomplish this has been done for us in and by Jesus Christ. Redemption is finished. It is an accomplished fact. And death, which is the wages of sin, has been overcome. Its terror has been removed by Jesus Christ who says to us, "I am the resurrection and the life. He that believes in me, though he were dead yet shall he live. And he that lives and believes in me shall never die." And with this he gives the promise, "Lo, I am with you always even unto the end of the world."

Christ makes it possible for us by faith in him as our Lord and Savior to see ourselves in our fallen, distorted condition and to have "courage to accept oneself as accepted in spite of being unacceptable."[3] We need not flee from God in fear; in his presence we can dare to be who we are: sinners—not fully human. We are able to come before him knowing and confessing "that we are by nature sinful and unclean and that we have sinned against him in thought, word and deed." We can do this because he has persuaded us that *"nevertheless"* he wants us and that we are his children by grace through faith in Jesus Christ. We are able to accept and confess the reality of our estrangement because we believe that it has been overcome by Christ who has reconciled us unto our Father.

This does not mean that we are now able to be the person God created us to be. The estrangement continues to evidence itself. But there is now the reality of "the flesh" and "the spirit." The omnipotent, defiant Ego remains. (Whenever we use ego to refer to man's egocentricity and sense of omnipotence, we will use the capital E in Ego.) But now we also pray, "Our Father" and "Thy will be done." We know we have been redeemed into loving relationship with God. He is now the "ultimate Person" in our lives. He is not only our Savior, but also our Lord, "in whom we live and move and have our being." This is now the ultimate relationship in life. And we are persuaded that nothing and no one can separate us from him and his love. Conscious of our egocentricity, omnipotence, hostility and defiance, we can accept these realities and experience his grace sufficient for us. In anxiety and loneliness, in joy and sorrow, in peace and guilt,

---

[3]Paul Tillich, *The Courage to Be* (New Haven: Yale U. Press), p. 164.

in faith and doubt, in love and hostility, in concern and indifference, in gain and loss, in plenty and want, in health and sickness, in life and death, he is our loving and faithful Lord, who enables us to grow in faith and hope and love. Acknowledging him as our life and salvation, we experience peace that passes human understanding and hope that abides.

Man is estranged not only from God but also from himself and other persons. He cannot fully be loved, love another, or himself as God created us for human love. By nature he now is hostile toward himself as well as toward God. Man has a tremendous capacity for self-hate because he subtly desires to be God and cannot be fully human. God in Christ accepts man in spite of this, but man cannot accept himself as completely as God accepts him. In this sense man cannot love and accept himself enough. Of course, love of oneself as a person does not here mean sinful self-love or egocentricity. Rather, it is self-esteem with the realization and acceptance of the fact that in spite of our not being fully human, we are still persons with dignity and individual worth who have been created by God and redeemed by Jesus Christ. In Christ, God makes it possible for us to believe this and as imperfect persons to experience his grace in living out our lives as *sons* of God. To be able to truly love ourselves as fully human persons created by God will be one of the fulfillments and joys in life eternal when the estrangement is completely removed.

And so it is also in man's relationship with his fellowman. Perfect love, which alone can completely resolve the human to human estrangement, does not exist in man. To "love thy neighbor as thyself" is just as impossible as to "love God with heart, soul, strength, and mind." Nevertheless, Jesus Christ confronts man with the words, "Love one another as I love you." By his grace such love, though imperfect, can be present and resolve the estrangement. The destructive anxiety of unresolved estrangement can be replaced by the healthy anxiety of resolved estrangement. The basic estrangement remains—the inability to be fully human in relationships—but because it is resolved in love, the anxiety that stems from it becomes the edge for spiritual and emotional growth.

because we are means of God's grace

Each of us needs to experience this kind of love in the human to human as well as in the divine to human relationship. Often when our teaching concerning God's love fails to take on meaningful reality in individual lives, it is because "experienced love" is not felt in the human to human relationships of those individuals.

The relationship of person to person is the horizontal dimension of the cross. An awareness of the vital, dynamic significance of this dimension has often been lacking within the Christian community. Jesus not only says, "Go into all the world and preach the Gospel." He also says, "A new commandment I give you, that you love one another as I love you. By this shall all men know that you are my disciples—will know me and the nature of my love—if you love one another as I love you."

Can a person meaningfully understand, know, and experience the love of God in Christ unless he has understood, known, and experienced love like that in the human relationship? Love, including the love of God, cannot be taught by verbal communication alone. It is impossible to comprehend God's love just by word without the Word becoming flesh and dwelling among us. So, also, the Word become flesh must become flesh in us. This is the basic insight in Luther's description of Christians as being "little Christs." Christ and his love must dwell in us richly. Without this we are, as Paul says, sounding brass and clanging cymbal as we seek to communicate the person and love of Jesus Christ.

We see the truth of all this in the life of a child. As the little child is taught that God loves him, he needs, according to God's design and command, to be experiencing this same kind of love which is, "I am loved because I am me"—within the basic human relationship of parent and child. Then, as he becomes aware on some level of his inability to be the person he was created to be, human love with understanding is essential to have him feel that *nevertheless* he is loved. He needs to feel "love like this" in the human relationship if he is also to have here "the courage to accept acceptance." Experiencing such love, the child does not have to deny or hide the fact of his imperfection, his omnipotent Ego, his egocentricity, hostility, and defiance. Because love is present he feels accepted and can in an imperfect way begin to accept himself as an imperfect person, in whom these realities exist. As he grows up, he gains the courage to face the realities of estrangement as a responsible person. God's grace in Christ makes this possible for him also in his relationships with others.

Then, too, the kind of limits that are placed on his life, the discipline and responsibility he receives, are as basic to love in the human relationship as in the relationship with God. Both the absence of limits, discipline, and responsibility so that the child always gets his way, or the presence of these essentially as an expression of hostility and rigidity communicate rejection, and the child grows up with unresolved feelings of egocentricity, omnipotence, hostility, defiance, insecurity, and inadequacy. But when love is the primary source of limits, discipline, and responsibility, these help to foster spiritual and emotional growth. Within the basic human relationship such love gives the child a sense of acceptance as an imperfect person. More than that, and of utmost importance, such a relationship enables the person to become aware of and begin to accept the fact that, being loved, he *nevertheless* is responsible for his feelings and behavior in relationship to God, himself, and others. With such acceptance, he is enabled to become a responsible, adult human being.

As we grow up in such a relationship we also learn to trust others. We let them know how we feel, and feel that they trust us. However, we also come to understand that none of these persons is the ultimate Person and none of these relationships with persons is the ultimate relationship. Our ultimate trust is in the Person, God, and the ultimate relationship is with God. Loved by God in Jesus Christ and by other persons, we by his grace have the capacity to love. We love him because he first loved us, and we are able to love ourselves and others because God and others have loved us.

Now how do these truths of our faith relate specifically to the alcoholic and his problem?

First of all, what about the fact of estrangement from God?

A number of recovered alcoholics whom we have met have what they feel is a very meaningful personal relationship with God. For some of them the relationship is that of the Christian faith. Others simply have "the feeling" of relationship with God which has come from some kind of spiritual awakening. However, Christian or otherwise, each of those with whom we have talked about this has said that prior to becoming an alcoholic he had no meaningful personal relationship with God. One man put it this way, "I used to be very religious but lacked any real spirituality." Many of these people came from what would be considered good church homes. They were baptized in the Christian faith, went to Sunday school, attended worship services, were instructed and confirmed. But none, even having been exposed to all this verbal communication, came to really believe and experience that God *really loved him* or *her*. Self continued as the controlling power, and the basic anxiety in life, that of man's estrangement from God, was unresolved.

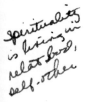

Second, when we seek to understand the alcoholic in his estrangement from self and others, we discover that here too the estrangement had not been meaningfully resolved. Prior to his alcoholism the alcoholic had no identity as a person. No matter what appearance he gave, he apparently never really felt loved and accepted by others as an imperfect person or accepted himself as an imperfect person. Much of the perfectionism we see in alcoholics stems from relationships in which they felt that they could not be loved apart from being perfect—however, that may have been perceived in relationship with a parent or parents. The basic human relationship in the alcoholic's life was usually authoritarian or overprotective and overpossessive. Sometimes the relationship was nonexistent because of the death of his parent or parents. (This kind of attempt at understanding is not an effort to make the parents, lack of parent, or what have you, the cause or scapegoat. The responsibility for the problem and its resolution still rests with the alcoholic.) The ego-centric, omnipotent, defiant, hostile self continued into adulthood as the controlling force and resulted in a situation in which the individual unconsciously wanted to be and tried to be someone he was not, someone that nobody is: namely, the superior, perfect One, God. He knew no peace within himself and was disillusioned by the lack of perfection in others. In a life he perceived as black and white he was confused in a world full of gray. In a real sense he never found his identity or experienced self-acceptance as an imperfect human being in an imperfect human race.

Anxiety over the unresolved estrangement in his human to human relationships was a consciously felt, not understood, powerfully destructive force. Alcohol temporarily removed the anxiety of this inner conflict. *[margin note: symptom]*

Why this person with this anxiety discovered alcohol rather than some other means of escape and experienced such tremendous relief from it remains the unanswered question. Others seeking escape from such anxiety may not try alcohol, or if they do, get no such relief from it. But at any rate, without understanding what was really causing the anxiety and what was really happening when he drank, he experienced that alcohol worked in a way that nothing or no one else ever had. *[margin note: families? habits?]*

With the anxiety of his estrangement anaesthetized by alcohol, he found himself "feeling good." He felt superior and omnipotent. This was living! Now he *was* somebody—identity. Being just another imperfect human being was intolerable because it didn't satisfy his need for perfection and omnipotence and was loaded with feelings of rejection. Alcohol worked wonders and it worked quickly. What it did "for" him he never forgot. He had the answer. Alcohol never let him down. Under the influence of alcohol the anxiety of estrangement in relationship to God, which he may or may not have been consciously aware of, was gone, as was the anxiety of estrangement from himself and others. In the unreal world of anaesthesia, he had a perception of himself that enabled him to accept *[margin note: gone from world]* himself, feel accepted by others, and feel quite adequate to face the realities of life.

Besides this anxiety relief through alcohol being immediate, he also felt relatively better after the drunk than he did before he started drinking. It appears that prior to drinking, the anxiety is severe, nameless, unexplainable. After the drunk, this kind of anxiety is gone. It is replaced by the anxiety of physical pain, guilt, remorse, and self-hatred. Such anxiety he can explain and tolerate more easily than the other. He feels he has it coming, and it also comes some time after the immediate relief from alcohol. Thus he unconsciously learns to evade the gnawing, vague anxiety of his unresolved estrangement.

In this light, we see the alcoholic seeking life in the sense that he is seeking to escape the anxiety of his estrangement. From the bottle he is attempting to resolve that which can ultimately be resolved only in Agape and human responsibility. Alcohol backfires on him. It becomes his master. As he seeks to save his own life he loses it. If the alcoholism goes unchecked, he will eventually end up living to drink and drinking to live, and that is death. Add to this tragic picture feelings of overwhelming guilt, fear, and loneliness, of feeling unloved, unwanted, not belonging, and we begin to sense the bondage and anguish of alcoholism.

Alcoholism is a "total sickness." The alcoholic is often physically sick, suffering from malnutrition because of eating improperly while drinking excessively. He is also emotionally, mentally, and socially sick. But as we try to understand the alcoholic within our Christian faith, we see him as a person who is also spiritually sick. The recovery program of A.A. makes it clear that this is the way many alcoholics feel about themselves, too.

What We Must Know About Ourselves

If we in the church are going to help these people, we must have not only some understanding of alcoholism but also an understanding of our own relationship with God. Even where our estrangement with God is overcome through his perfect love by faith in Jesus Christ, there still is egocentricity, omnipotence, hostility, and defiance. And with this there is pretense and mask-wearing before him as we carry along our scapegoats to avoid personal responsibility for our feelings and behavior. All too often, and without even knowing it, we come to God as we think we ought to be or as we like to think we are, rather than as we really are. We can so easily imagine ourselves more sinful or less sinful than some other person—and quite often less sinful than the alcoholic.

In reality there is still that in each of us which will not and cannot fully let God be God, that which prevents us from loving and trusting him "with all our heart," that which crucifies him anew each day. Each of us is "a chief of sinners" in God's sight. There is no other kind. No person is less sinful or more sinful than another. If an alcoholic were not an alcoholic, he would be just as sinful a person. Those of us who are not alcoholic are just as sinful as we would be if we were alcoholic. We are all in need of God's grace. And there are no degrees of need for grace. John, the beloved disciple of Jesus, and the adulterous woman needed the same grace for the same basic sinfulness. When we realize and truly accept this truth, we see that the alcoholic is not someone unlike ourselves but *our brother* in sinfulness and need. He is one of us. Our relationship with him ceases to be marred by moralism.

There also remains our estrangement from ourselves and one another because of the lack of perfect love. The "omnipotent-egocentric Ego" continues to express itself in various ways—in hostility, pride, selfishness, dishonesty, insecurity, mistrust, indifference, and self-pity. These and other painful realities we often try to cover up or escape from by various defense mechanisms. We may pretend it isn't so, pretend to feel and be someone we are not. We may rationalize, providing a reason other than the real reason for our feeling and behavior, a reason outside ourselves. We may project our own feelings onto another person so that we see that person as being hostile, for instance, instead of ourselves. We may hide in the group, losing identity and avoiding responsibility as individuals by conforming to the ideas and behavior of others. We may escape through extreme busyness with something else or through withdrawing from the situations and relationships in which we experience painful feelings. Or we may repress these realities from conscious awareness. Such mechanisms are at work in us to protect us from the reality of our condition. They allow us to present ourselves to ourselves in a way which, though phony, we hope will enable us to accept ourselves better and to feel others will accept us better too. They are also mechanisms to avoid responsibility for our own feelings and behavior. These, of course, are not thought-out conscious processes. They are very similar to what is taking place when the alcoholic reaches for that first drink.

It is right here that the nature of the fellowship of the church as a loving, understanding, accepting, responsible fellowship is of vital importance. In this fellowship, established by Christ himself, there is to be an awareness of our common sinfulness, weaknesses, problems, and responsibility. Here there is to be a "feeling" communication that gets through to the person—a communication of understanding and acceptance of one another in our estrangement. Within this fellowship people are to feel free to be essentially as they are. They don't have to be pretenders. They don't have to deny the realities of estrangement. Unfortunately, many individuals don't ever do this, and what is more unfortunate, we often fortify their defenses against essentially being themselves with distorted ideas as to how "church people" are to feel and behave. Although in the Christian fellowship there should be the openness to understand and the capacity to accept every person as he is, the fellowship is sometimes a hindrance rather than a help for man in the pain of his estrangement.

Within our fellowship there commonly exist distorted images of who a Christian is—and what a Christian is like—images that give believers reasons to wear masks and live in pretense.

For instance, there is the emphasis on sins instead of sin, and even some so-called sins aren't even sins. It can be easy to confess sins. It is quite a different matter to become aware of and accept the nature of the sin concerning which the sins are but certain expressions.

For instance, it is much easier for a married man to confess "the sin" of a sexual affair with another woman, than to become aware of and confess "the basic nature of the sin"—which may have the qualities of egocentricity, hostility, resentment, self-pity, with a high degree of emotional irresponsibility in relationship to God, himself and others—and realize that his affair was only one expression through many years of self-deception.

Or it is easier to confess "the sin" of being too concerned about others and not concerned enough about one's own family than to become aware of and confess "the nature of the sin" which is really caring essentially only about oneself—the impression others have of you—the public image—the reality of unresolved estrangement. There are "images of sinfulness" within the church that readily enable people to remain unaware of their sin and basically irresponsible.

Another common image of distortion is that Christians will always be "strong in the Lord." Consequently, the individual may be caused to feel more guilty than ever about his weakness and his need for help. He is led to feel that if he were really a Christian, he wouldn't be so weak and so overwhelmed by trouble. The fellowship should enable us to accept the reality of our weakness, to function responsibly in seeking help when necessary, to be ready to face the problem responsibly, and to experience the truth that God's strength is perfected in our weakness. But where the distorted image exists, a troubled believer in need of help may feel an even greater need to put on the mask and "pretend it isn't so."

Another related truth within the fellowship is that Christ is our victorious Lord and that, therefore, the Christian is joyful, hopeful, and victorious in every situation of life. If, in the communication of this truth, the realities of doubt and grief are not included, a distorted image results. The believer may be led to feel even more guilty than he already does about real doubt or grief, and may come to the point of having to deny it or cover it up. Doubt and grief are real. Within the fellowship we are to be enabled to accept our doubts and our grief, but we do not have to doubt as those who have no faith or grieve as those who have no hope. Doubt and grief are not a negation of our hope and victory in Christ—our Lord as man experienced and expressed doubt and grief. Yet how difficult it is for some believers, because of a distorted image, to accept and express their doubt and grief.

Then, too, there can be a distorted communication within the fellowship in regard to love. It is true that Christians are to love, not hate. But a distorted image results unless this communication includes the fact that nevertheless Christians will have hostile feelings and not always love as they ought. To deny or cover up this fact is harmful for the individual and for the group. The Scriptures take for granted that we will have hostile feelings, but provides this admonition: Don't let the sun go down upon your anger. Hostility denied, covered up, and not resolved turns into resentment that isolates and consumes the person. The fellowship, in only communicating what ought to be, hinders people from being free to accept what is. It is only through awareness, acceptance, expression, and finally confession that the grace of Christ's forgiveness and his power to transform hostility into love can be experienced.

Another truth of Christian life is that Christians are not to hurt people, but to love and help them. This truth is also liable to distortion if we ignore the fact that love sometimes will hurt people because love confronts them with reality. Jesus in love confronted people and in the process they were hurt, but not harmed. This was necessary, as he in love sought to help them see the truth about themselves. One person said, "A man has to love and care an awful lot to confront me with the truth about myself as he did."

It is disturbing to see how often the fellowship even as it confesses that "we are by nature sinful" says in effect to its members, "If you are really Christians you won't commit this or that sin; you won't be selfish or hostile." Unless the fellowship of saints, which is simply the fellowship of believers, can truly be the fellowship of sinners—of the imperfect—it will not know the glory of being the fellowship of the redeemed here and now. Without this, we will all the more pretend, deny, and try to cover up our basic sinfulness and weakness; we will never experience the freedom to essentially be ourselves in the presence of God, and one another.

Together with the words "you shall not" there must be within the fellowship the words "nevertheless you will." For this impossible reality of our estrangement there is Jesus Christ whose grace is sufficient. In him there is transforming love and power that gives us the "courage to be"[4] in such reality and to grow in faith, love, and obedience as responsible persons.

Besides these mechanisms we use to deny or escape the anxiety of our estrangement, we should also understand that there are many addictions other than alcohol that result from escaping anxiety.

A person may become a "success addict." In such a man we see the same powerlessness and irresponsibility that we see in the alcoholic, but for him the overwhelming compulsion is to be successful. Success handles the anxiety of his estrangement as he strives for acceptance. The defiant egocentric self is in control, and success is his bondage just as drinking is for the alcoholic.

In varying degrees the desire for success exists in many of us, maybe not as an addiction, but as an evidence of estrangement. Often the "I must be successful" is more a reality than the freedom to be faithful. The first is an effort to escape or resolve estrangement by one's own achievements: man's effort to heal himself. The second is the grace of God in which estrangement is resolved in love. The Bible does not talk of success, but it does talk of faithfulness.

Here it is interesting to note how the church has adopted many of the success symbols of our materialistic, secularistic culture and is feeding this basic problem of man from which Christ has come to

---

[4]Tillich, *op. cit.*

set us free. We have images of the successful pastor and the successful congregation. In terms of these, there can be great success with little faithfulness as far as the real meaning of a pastoral ministry is concerned. On the other hand, there can be great faithfulness where the symbols of success are few or none at all. The pastor who has strong success needs in terms of these symbols of bigness, and has "succeeded," may have little awareness of the anxiety of estrangement that drives him; and whatever the "success," he is driven to still greater "success." If this compulsion eventually leads to a nervous breakdown, we usually attribute it to overwork rather than recognizing it as the result of an addiction for which he, like the alcoholic, needs help.

The faithful pastor, on the other hand, is not driven by these success needs. The anxiety of his estrangement has been resolved in a more meaningful way and there is freedom for faithfulness. Nevertheless, he is still aware that the problem exists because he recognizes the dual reality of the desire to be faithful over against the need to be successful within himself and in relationship to his congregation, fellow pastors, and the church. In many cases the church, with its success oriented thinking, is not assisting him in his desire to be faithful.

Often "work addiction" goes together with "success addiction," but it perhaps need not be so. A person may be a "work addict" simply because the anxiety of estrangement is escaped by overworking, keeping himself unreasonably busy. Many who aren't work addicts have experienced how busyness reduces anxiety. The work addict has an uncontrollable compulsion to work. His wife may express it by saying he is "married to his work." She and the children see little of him. If he takes a vacation, he probably can't enjoy it unless he can keep himself extremely busy. When and if he is at home, he still isn't at home in terms of meaningful relationship with his wife and children. He is preoccupied, tense, going through the motions of being involved, but "his heart really isn't in it." Work does for him something that it doesn't do for others in handling the anxiety of estrangement, just as alcohol does for the alcoholic.

Let's talk about pastors again. The particular pastor we have in mind is the one who preaches a beautiful Mother's Day sermon about the family being a gift of God, but whose own family seldom sees him. His wife can't understand it. What she hears him preach isn't evidenced in their home. She is lonely and hurt and has had to try to find other outlets because her need for a meaningful personal relationship with her husband is, for all practical purposes, going unmet. Their children need not only her; they need their father also, but he has little or no time for really being a father to his children. They have, at best, very little family life. She doesn't object to the fact that he is busy. This she understands. But she knows he could be at home more often *if he really wanted to be.* When she tries to talk about this and share her feelings with him he says, "I'm doing this for the Lord's sake and this is a sacrifice we have to make." Even the alcoholic can't come up with a rationalization that good! And like the alcoholic, who initially never feels better than when he is under the anaesthesia of alcohol, the work addict never feels better than when he works compulsively. Like the alcohol and success addict, so the work addict is quite incapable of truly meaningful relationships.

We might look at this one a little more closely. An alcoholic is in the hospital following a drinking binge. In the room next to him is a work addict who, because of overwork and the underlying anxiety that is driving him, has had a heart attack. Each has the same doctor, a man who doesn't understand the phenomenon of addiction. The doctor says to the alcoholic, "You have to quit your drinking. If you can't quit, then don't drink so much when you drink. Take it easy." To the work addict he says, "You have been overdoing it, you are driving yourself too hard in your work. You need to work, but you have to quit overdoing it. Take it easy."

Sometime later, after both have left the hospital, the alcohol addict is back to his compulsive drinking and the work addict to his compulsive working. Each ends up in the hospital again. This time the doctor says to the alcoholic, "You are going to kill yourself if you keep this up." He says the same to the work addict. And that is just what happens.

In the papers we read the notice of the death of the alcoholic. If we know him, we react by saying or thinking, "What a horrible way to die." And it is. However, for the work addict, whose addiction has perhaps resulted in great visible accomplishment, not only in his work, but also in his community and church, there is a quite different kind of attitude, reaction, and obituary. How many are aware that underneath the excessive, uncontrolled working was the same unresolved anxiety of estrangement that was underneath the excessive, uncontrolled drinking? What alcohol did for this anxiety in one person, work did for the same anxiety in the other.

Another common addiction is "food addiction," one of the results being obesity. Many people who are not food addicts experience some of this reality when they are trying to watch their waistlines, and in anxious moments find themselves going to the refrigerator to take in high calorie foods, such as a chocolate sundae. They have unconsciously learned that such intake takes the edge off their anxiety. But some people in eating get tremendous relief for anxiety, just as some people do in drinking, and become "food addicts." Many times the "food addict" may be dieting in public but compulsively overeating in secret. If there is an actual period of dieting, it is like the "water wagon" experience of the alcoholic. During such a strict diet period the person will suffer from great anxiety that isn't consciously experienced when he is compulsively eating. He is terribly miserable. If he tries a specific dietary aid for a while he will always eat without control again, as the alcoholic will drink without control again. With many food addicts, food works so well in regard to this basic anxiety that we even have the image of the "happy, jolly, fat person." The food addict sneaks his food, gulps his food, and minimizes the amount he eats, just as the alcoholic does with his drinking. And like the alcoholic, he is just as dishonest in his thinking and feels the same intense feelings of guilt, shame, and remorse. But as we know, this is much more respectable, and there is little awareness that basically the nature of the problem is like unto that of the person who has become addicted to alcohol.

In many of our lives, that which will buy things or things themselves do something to relieve our anxiety. Because we can temporarily reduce our anxiety in this way, we have difficulty in beholding the birds and the lilies, how God cares for them, and seeking first the kingdom of God and its righteousness knowing that these things will be added unto us. Much of our buying is anxiety reduction behavior. Some people even develop an addiction to acquiring and consequently continually need something new. Closely related to this are the "pleasure addicts," who compulsively seek out pleasure to escape their inner restlessness.

For a final example, there is the addiction that is moralism or legalism. This handles the anxiety so well that even Christ couldn't reach the Pharisees. It is interesting to note that these are the only people with whom Christ became harsh. "If I am so good by what I do or don't do, then how can God help loving me, how can I help loving myself and being loved by others?" On the conscious level this person has resolved the estrangement. He thinks he is whole. He needs no Savior. As an escape, his addiction works much better for him than alcohol does for the alcoholic. When the alcoholic sobers up, there is guilt, shame, remorse, a sense of wrongness and hopelessness. Legalism works so well that consciously the legalist doesn't really have these feelings, even though he has to work hard at his legalism to keep these feelings from coming to the surface.

Perhaps one of the greatest evidences of our common estrangement is our inability to glorify God, even after we have prayed that it might be so. Just a little word of praise after the task is completed and so easily we can automatically, silently, sometimes not so silently, step out in front of God to take the glory unto ourselves. Because we are estranged we need praise. It communicates acceptance and a sense of worth. But our estrangement is so great that we rarely can receive praise without in some way blocking the glory of God. A friend pointed up the dilemma in another way when he said, "Have you ever done anything good for someone else and never told another person?" Even the inability to accept praise is a subtle way of blocking the glory of God. No wonder the Scriptures and saints declare that the glorification of God is the highest expression of Christian faith—of the resolution of the anxiety of our estrangement.

All of this about ourselves—our tendency to distort Christian truth, our defense mechanisms, our addictions—should not surprise us. It is all part of what we are saying when we confess that we are by nature sinful. Because we were created for perfect loving relationship, the crucial question for us as estranged persons, persons who cannot be who we were created to be, is whether or not we have a meaningful personal redemptive relationship with Christ as Lord and Savior, and whether or not we are able to live in meaningful personal relationship with ourselves and others, particularly with the members of our own family. The person we are at home is closest to the real "me." Many persons, including those who are trapped by certain kinds of addictions, are in a bondage that makes meaningful relationships impossible. Their bondage is involvement, conscious or unconscious, in an effort to save their own lives, to overcome their own estrangement. The Gospel makes clear that only the person who has by *grace* experienced the resolution of estrangement with God, himself, and others is free to live as a responsible person, in humility of spirit in meaningful relationships that find expression in service to God and man.

It is important for us to grow in awareness of the realities of our own estrangement and the sufficiency of God's grace. The story is told of the retired pastor who, looking back upon his ministry, divided it into three phases. In the first phase the people were in the river and he was on the bank telling them how to get out of the water and up on the bank where he was. In the second phase he was on the edge of the bank reaching down and out to help the people get up on the bank where he was. In the third phase, the phase of real wisdom and understanding, he ministered with the realization that he was in the river with the people, they were holding him up, he was holding them up, and underneath them all were the everlasting arms of God.

We, too, must be in this phase if we are going to be of help to alcoholics. When Christ was on earth he became totally who we are. This is Agape. In loving one another as he loves us, we do not have to become who or what the other person is. That we already are, and of this fact we need to be aware. Such self-knowledge and acceptance helps us to realize that the alcoholic's problem underneath the drinking is our problem. Who he is, we are. What he feels, we feel to some degree. By nature we are truly his brothers in estrangement.

It is this kind of attitude and understanding about ourselves that makes possible understanding and acceptance in relationship with the alcoholic. Unconsciously he is looking for this in others in their relationships with him. He doesn't expect to find it and experience it. And when he finds it in a pastor, strangely enough in many cases the last person he expected to have it, this can be a delightful surprise and readily result in the lowering of his defenses and the beginning of a meaningful helping relationship in which the alcoholic can begin to face the reality of his problem responsibly.

II.

PROGRESSIVE SYMPTOMS
OF
ALCOHOLISM

In understanding the alcoholism most common in the United States and helping alcoholics, it is important to know the progressive symptoms as developed by Dr. E. M. Jellinek. These include the distinguishing marks between problem drinking (considered by some to be a form of alcoholism, but not so considered here) and alcoholism. Every symptom need not appear in every alcoholic, nor do the symptoms necessarily appear in the specific order listed.

As mentioned earlier, we have here a classic description of the truth that as a man seeks to save his life he loses it. Clear in the symptoms also is the presence of guilt. As the alcoholism progresses, the alcoholic feels more and more that there is no hope in God because of the way he feels about himself and because he sees God only as the Moralist. This can easily lead to agnosticism. He may intellectually question the existence of God—if there is a God, why doesn't he get him out of his dilemma? But deeper within he may find it emotionally necessary to question God's existence because he feels that if there is a God, surely God cannot accept him.

A pastor may feel that verbal communication of the love of God early in the relationship should take care of this, but experience proves that it doesn't. The reasons for this are discussed in detail in the section on "counseling the alcoholic."

Pre-Alcoholism Stage

The pre-alcoholic phase is marked by (a) more drinking episodes and (b) more drinking at each episode. The person begins to drink more heavily and more often than his friends. "Getting drunk" becomes a habit.

Many excessive drinkers never go beyond this point, but for many others these are ominous signs indicating that alcoholism lies ahead. At this point there may be lack of awareness of what is happening, but more likely, lack of meaningful concern about the change in drinking. He is just having "more fun more often." Actually he may already be developing a strong need for the pampering effects of sedative alcohol to relieve anxiety.

Early Stage

(1) Blackout. This is the first real "danger signal" as far as alcoholism is concerned. It is not to be confused with "passing out." He doesn't pass out from drinking, but when he awakens the next morning he may only recall the evening before up to a certain point or only parts of the evening. This can be laughed off as the result of "hanging on a good one" or can cause quite a bit of concern. People who aren't alcoholics may have blackouts. A person may get drunk just once in his lifetime and have a blackout. However, in people moving toward alcoholism the blackouts tend to develop a pattern. During a blackout a person may appear to be functioning quite normally, even drive an automobile safely home from quite a distance, but not be able to recall any of this.

(2) Sneaking drinks. The sedative effect of alcohol begins to be the primary reason for drinking. This is a significant and dangerous change. One evidence of this is the sneaking of drinks because he wants to feel the sedative effect sooner and wants more than the others are going to drink. He may have some before he goes to the party, or at the party offer to mix the drinks in order to get a few extra while he is in the kitchen and load his drink with a larger quantity of alcohol, or excuse himself to go to the bathroom where he makes use of the hidden bottle. If we think of drinking as the partaking of a beverage and the social aspects of drinking, this per-

son doesn't want to drink. He wants to imbibe sedation. It just happens that the sedation he wants is in liquid form. Such sneaking activity is also an indication that the amount he wants to drink and is drinking bothers him even though he would deny this. He feels guilty and therefore sneaks his extra drinks.

(3) Preoccupation with alcohol. While at work he may well be thinking about and waiting to get his drinks at noon and/or on the way home. When going to a party, he wants to know if there will be alcohol. Drinking alcohol is synonymous with having a good time, all the time. If drinking is not going to be part of the activity he may not be interested.

(4) Gulping first drinks. Here is another evidence that his inbibing of alcohol is not drinking. He gulps those first drinks because he has learned that this is the quickest way to "feel it," to get the effect of the sedation. He is "the man with the empty glass."

(5) Guilt about drinking. His drinking is no longer "normal" and he consciously feels guilty. The nature of the guilt feeling here is different from any other previous guilt he may have felt about his drinking. It is now related to the fact that his drinking and his primary reasons for drinking have changed and no longer fit the norms of his previous drinking.

(6) Avoiding conversation about alcohol. This naturally follows the guilt feeling. Whereas he perhaps used to get a bang out of talking about his intoxication after the weekend party, now he not only wants to avoid talking about it, but may get irritated if someone else does. He is afraid they will talk about "his drinking."

(7) Proportion of blackouts to drinking episodes increases. At this point it is believed that the person can still quit by the force of sheer will-power if there is sufficient awareness and motivation, or by getting help to understand and resolve the underlying conflicts and anxiety. However, most people who reach this point don't want to quit drinking or change their drinking behavior while they still

can. Later, if and when they want to quit, they no longer are able to do so. Many have already lost control.

Middle Stage

(8) Loss of control. This initially is loss of control over the amount that he drinks. He can't predict what will happen after he takes the first drink. He may take just a drink or two, or he may drink without control. Usually he drinks without control. Intending to have a couple on the way home from work, he is still at the bar at closing time. He plans not to get drunk at the party and gets drunk. Never again, on the basis of what is now known, will he be able to be a controlled drinker. As the alcoholism progresses he will also lose control over the time when he drinks and thus drink when he doesn't plan to drink. He reaches the point where he literally can't keep from drinking or control the amount he drinks. He is totally powerless over alcohol. Some, perhaps more than we think, experienced loss of control in their initial drinking experiences. Others do not experience this phenomenon until they have had many years of controlled drinking.

(9) Rationalizing and alibis. He feels guilty and defensive about his loss of control and the drunkenness that results. As we so often do with our behavior, he begins to rationalize. He erects an elaborate system of "reasons" for drinking the way he does, partly to answer family and associates, but primarily to reassure and fool himself. It is an automatic process requiring no effort to think up excuses. He is never at a loss to find a reason other than the real reason, loss of control, of which he very likely is not aware. Rarely, if ever, will he say that he just likes to get drunk, because rarely does he plan to get drunk. This bewilders him. He doesn't want anybody to know that he can't figure out why he consistently gets drunk when he drinks. "The idea that somehow, someday he will be able to control and enjoy his drinking is the great obsession of every

abnormal drinker. The persistence of this illusion is astonishing. Many pursue it into the gates of insanity or death."

(10) Social pressures increase. Because of the nature of his drinking, pressures increase from wife, friends, employer, and others. This is painful, but to preserve his self-esteem and ease his guilt, he reinforces the rationalization system. Most of the people in the picture possibly won't be aware either of the real reason he is drinking to intoxication. They may be telling him he has to use his will power and quit, or at least not drink so much. They reinforce the delusion that enables the alcoholic to keep from facing the reality of powerlessness or loss of control.

(11) Grandiose behavior. He starts buying things he doesn't need, maybe the very best, runs up bills, picks up the checks at the restaurant, leaves big tips. He is the big shot. This is another way to avoid the truth about himself and his condition.

(12) Aggressive behaviors. Because he believes that other people are the fault of his troubles, he strikes out against them with verbal abuse, sometimes even with physical abuse. Early evidences of physical abuse usually indicate an underlying severe disorder. Such abuse in the latter stages of alcoholism is frequently and essentially an expression of his self-hatred projected upon someone else.

(13) Persistent remorse and guilt. Now he can't throw it off as easily as before. There is a persistent awareness of what he has been doing to himself and others. While others may condemn him, he is his worst condemner. This will often lead him back to the bottle only to discover that the nagging remorse and guilt are still there after the alcohol is removed.

(14) "Water Wagon." This is the great attempt to "quit on his own." A period of time is usually set. If he makes it through this period, he has proved to himself that he can quit even though he then proceeds to drink and get drunk. If the compulsion to drink gets too strong before the time he set is up, a "good excuse" can

be found. Since he doesn't disapprove of drinking why should he go on the "water wagon" if he really believes his drinking is no problem? The "water wagon" is obvious evidence of a severe drinking problem, but the alcoholic sees it as proving that he doesn't have a problem.

(15) Changing patterns of drinking behavior. Under pressure from others and within himself, he tries to break the hold alcohol has on him. He sets up rules as to when and what he will drink. He isn't going to drink alone any more, or in the afternoon, or during the week, or any hard liquor, just beer. But this doesn't work. The problem is clearly revealed as not being when or what or with whom he drinks, but simply loss of control.

(16) Social relationships drop. This is hard on his self-esteem, but automatically he finds a reason other than himself and his drinking for this painful development. What a bunch of "hypocrites" those people are! He may drop them before they drop him. With this comes the establishment of relationships on another level where people are drinking in his pattern. When he recovers, it is a painful discovery to see that his "real friends" were "drinking friends" and nothing more.

(17) Loss of job. This either happens because he is fired or smart enough to see it coming and quit before he was fired. If the latter, he can say that he never lost a job because of drinking which in his mixed-up thinking means he isn't an alcoholic.

(18) Drinking becomes of *central* importance in behavior. Whereas he previously sought to keep his drinking from interfering with his primary responsibilities and interests in life, now his drinking interferes with these, too. He is completely captive to alcohol.

(19) Narrowing range of interests. Life is narrowing slowly but surely to himself and the bottle. Last year he went hunting with the fellows but didn't get his gun out of the case because he got drunk. This year he didn't even go on the annual hunting trip.

(20) Reinterpretation of personal relations. He has the need to explain why he has established new relationships on a lower level without facing up to his drinking as a real cause.

(21) Marked self-pity. He feels everybody is against him, nobody cares—poor me.

(22) Geographic escape. The problem is the neighborhood, town, or state where he is living, his job, his in-laws living in the same town, or something else about the *place*. The answer is to move and get away from it all. Having moved or changed jobs, he still gets drunk.

(23) Changing family activities. The family may leave him or realize that they have to plan their life and activities apart from him. They can never count on him.

(24) Unreasonable resentments. These make it almost intolerable for anyone to live with him. Such resentments are projections of his own intense self-hatred and guilt. Quite often the wife is the target and such behavior is "par for the course."

(25) Protecting supply. He has to make sure there is enough to drink and that nobody removes or destroys his supply. This can be quite humorous, as well as desperate, as he cleverly seeks out the safest hiding places.

(26) Neglect of nutrition. With the severity of his drinking comes decrease in appetite. He drinks and doesn't eat. Although appearing well nourished, he may be suffering malnutrition.

(27) First hospitalization. Weakened physically and unable now to get off the drinking, he has to be hospitalized. When released, he may begin to feel like a new man. There may be the thought, "Never again!" He feels fine. Drinking is no problem.

(28) Alcoholic jealousy. Suspicion develops toward his wife. This is an expression of his own feelings of guilt and inadequacy. The verbal abuse and accusations can be very severe and puzzling for a faithful wife.

(29) Decrease in sexual desire. This is self-explanatory. Should it occur, the wife may become quite concerned. She should know that quite often this is just part of the progression of alcoholism and it will be corrected in his recovery.

(30) Morning drink. The morning drink takes care of the hangover—jitters, guilt, remorse, depression. He needs it to "start the day right." This initiates the cycle of continuous drinking and speeds up the progression of the alcoholism.

Late Stage

(31) Binge and bender. Now he drinks for several days, completely helpless. There is utter disregard for family, job, everything. To get more liquor he will lie, pawn his possessions, even steal. The binge leaves him a shaking, frightened, guilt-ridden person. "Never again"—but then comes the next one.

(32) Ethical deterioration. The exercise of moral decisions deteriorates because of lack of use, compulsive drinking, and downward progression of his alcoholism. The only remedy: more liquor.

(33) Reversible deterioration in thinking. His ability to think clearly is impaired through sedation and disuse of his brain functions. People begin to wonder if he has become mentally ill. This reverses itself in his recovery.

(34) Alcoholic psychosis. This can be a temporary psychotic episode or permanent brain damage.

(35) Social deterioration in drinking companions. He is now near or at skid row level in regard to his drinking pattern, environment, and drinking companions. Skid row may be avoided if he has sufficient money to sustain his drinking.

(36) Alcohol beverage substitutes. If he can't get alcoholic beverages he will use bay rum, shaving lotion, canned heat, rubbing alcohol, etc.

(37) Decrease in amounts consumed. Because of physical deterior-

ation, drinking smaller amounts of alcohol will result in a higher degree of blood alcohol concentration than in the past.

(38) Indefinable fears. Now he is totally frightened by nameless fears he cannot remove. He feels a sense of impending doom and destruction. Nervous, shaky, he is unable to face life without alcohol.

(39) Tremors (persistent). He develops the "shakes," a serious nervous condition. He may have delirium tremens, which is the onset of persistent shaking, trembling, and confusion accompanied by horrible hallucinations. This is an extremely terrifying experience, the cause of which is not fully understood. DT's can be fatal. If an alcoholic, after a binge, is to be hospitalized and there will be a delay, it is best to see that he has a supply of alcohol to avoid DT's.

(40) Psycho-motor inhibitions. The alcoholic lacks sufficient coordination to do the most simple physical function without alcohol.

(41) Obsessive drinking to remove alcoholic symptoms.

(42) Vague religious drives. The reality of his problem strikes. He is desperate. Maybe religion will bring him out of it.

(43) Collapse of rationalization system and admission of condition and personal defeat. No longer can he make excuses for himself or put the blame on others. He accepts the fact of his powerlessness. He can no longer deceive himself. "I need help and I want help." This is surrender.

(44) Solitary drinking (may appear at any point in the progression).

These progressive symptoms make it obvious that the alcoholic is deeply troubled in his drinking and experiences severe inner anguish. It is the story not only of progression but also of struggle. He is either struggling to quit or control his drinking while at the same time doing battle to keep from seeing and accepting his powerlessness.

Because of what is known about alcoholism today and particularly because of the work of A.A., many alcoholics go through the surrender phenomenon in the crucial phase or in the early part of the chronic phase.

Let us not glibly think that the alcoholic should somehow automatically be able to see and accept his powerlessness very early in the progression. We know ourselves better than that. We know the ease with which we provide strong rationalizations to keep ourselves from looking at and accepting some of the problems and weaknesses of our own lives. Everything within the alcoholic struggles against accepting the reality of his problem. The surrender comes only through pain and conflict resulting from his problem and in relationships of understanding and acceptance where he can come to accept the reality of his powerlessness and know that there is help for him as there has been for thousands of others.

It is important for us to understand and emotionally accept that these are *symptoms* of the illness of alcoholism, just as an elevated temperature is a symptom of an infection. Obviously, it is more difficult to perceive and accept these symptoms as symptoms of the illness of alcoholism, because they are essentially behavioral, create such problems, and progressively make any kind of meaningful relationship, communication, and planning with the alcoholic, not yet ready for help, quite impossible. But this does make clear the need for truly accepting alcoholism as an illness.

It is apparent from these progressive symptoms that the alcoholic is totally sick—mentally, emotionally, physically, socially, and spiritually, and that he progressively becomes more sick in the totality of his being and relationships.

There is a theory that seems to be validated in clinical experience that even while the alcoholic is apparently recovering with sobriety in all areas of his life, the illness, in some mysterious way, continues to progress during his years of sobriety. This means that if he has ten years of sobriety and then starts drinking again, he will begin not where he left off in the progression, but in a short time will be where he would have been had he continued drinking during that ten-year period. Seldom do we see an alcoholic who recovers again if he starts drinking again after a number of years of sobriety.

So far we have referred to the alcoholic as "male." The ratio of male alcoholics to female alcoholics seems to be narrowing. In some settings it looks like the ratio is fifty-fifty. The female alcoholic is apt to experience more intense shame and often will remain the "hidden alcoholic" for a longer period of time, as she does most of her drinking within the home and is protected by her husband through denial or cover-up.

Finally, it should be noted that there is in these progressive symptoms a set of "thinking and feeling" about one's drinking that together with the symptoms are of real value in detection of the presence of alcoholism. Prior to alcoholism, if the person wanted to have a drink or drink excessively, he just did it. Now there is defensiveness, denial, minimization, and the obvious need to explain the drinking behavior. This "thinking and feeling" set within the alcoholic is readily perceived when there has been active involvement with alcoholics who are still drinking, and by listening to recovered alcoholics talk about their drinking behavior.

III.

ALCOHOLICS ANONYMOUS

The greatest number of recovered alcoholics have been restored to sobriety within the fellowship of Alcoholics Anonymous. This group traces its beginnings to 1934, when a man by the name of Bill found his way up and out to sobriety through a dramatic, intense spiritual experience which involved surrender to God in his powerlessness.

Bill had a friend, Ebby, who was a member of the Oxford Group. At one time they had been drinking companions, and Bill had marked Ebby as a hopeless case. One day while Bill was drinking, Ebby came to see him. Ebby was sober. When Bill asked what had happened, Ebby explained what he had received from the Oxford Group. He had learned that he had to admit he was licked and that he ought to take stock of himself and confess his defects to another person in confidence. He had learned, too, that he needed to make restitution for harm done to others, to practice the kind of giving that has no price tag on it—the giving of himself to somebody—and finally to pray to God for power to help him do all this. If he did not believe there was a God, then he was told to pray to whatever God there "might be."[1]

Ebby didn't pressure Bill, but Bill could not forget what he had heard. His moods continued to swing from rebellion against God to hope and then back again

Later, during hospitalization to sober up, Bill was very depressed. Ebby showed up again. Bill asked him to repeat his formula, which Ebby did. The depression, according to Bill, deepened unbearably

---

[1] *Alcoholics Anonymous Comes of Age,* A. A. Publishing, Inc., p. 59.

until he seemed to be at the bottom of the pit. He still gagged on the idea of a power greater than himself, but for the moment his proud obstinacy was crushed. All at once he found himself crying out, "If there is a God, let Him show Himself! I am ready to do anything, anything!"[2]

Bill describes his experience in the following manner:

"Suddenly the room lit up with a great white light. I was caught up into an ecstasy which there are no words to describe. It seemed to me, in my mind's eye, that I was on a mountain and that a wind not of air but of spirit was blowing. And then it burst upon me that I was a free man. Slowly the ecstasy subsided. I lay on the bed, but now for a time I was in another world, a new world of consciousness. All about me and through me there was a wonderful feeling of Presence and I thought to myself, 'So this is the God of the preacher!' A great peace stole over me and I thought, 'No matter how wrong things seem to be, they still are right. Things are all right with God and His world.'

"Then little by little, I began to be frightened. My modern education crawled back and said to me, 'You are hallucinating. You had better get the doctor.' Dr. Silkworth asked me a lot of questions. After a while he said, 'No, Bill, you are not crazy. There has been some basic psychological or spiritual event here. I've read about these things in books. Sometimes spiritual experiences do release people from alcoholism.' Immensely relieved, I fell again to wondering what actually had happened.

"More light on this came the next day. It was Ebby, I think, who brought me a copy of William James's *Varieties of Religious Experience*. It was rather difficult reading for me, but I devoured it from cover to cover. Spiritual experiences, James thought, could have objective reality; almost like gifts from the blue, they could transform people. Some were sudden brilliant illuminations; others came on very gradually. Some flowed out of religious channels; others did not. But nearly all had the great common denominators

Ibid., p. 63.

of pain, suffering, and calamity. Complete hopelessness and deflation at depth were almost required to make the recipient ready. The significance of all this burst upon me. Deflation at depth—yes, that was it. Exactly that happened to me."[3]

In another writing Bill has this to say in connection with that experience. "There I humbly offered myself to God, as I then understood Him, to do with me as He would. I placed myself unreservedly under His care and direction. I admitted for the first time that of myself I was nothing; that without Him I was lost. I ruthlessly faced my sins and became willing to have my new-found Friend take them away, root and branch. I have not had a drink since."[4]

The complete story of Bill's life and recovery along with the story of A.A. can be read in the two books, *Alcoholics Anonymous* and *Alcoholics Anonymous Comes of Age*. The end result was a gradual increase in sober alcoholics through Bill and others who shared what they had experienced and what had worked for them. Today there are approximately 300,000 alcoholics in A.A.

Within this understanding and accepting fellowship that communicates so meaningfully to the alcoholic in his alcoholism and estrangement, the basic principles suggested for recovery are simple but extremely profound. Emphasis is not on "Why did I become an alcoholic?" but rather on *"What must I do as a responsible person* to gain sobriety and be able to face life meaningfully without alcohol?" The principles are spelled out in what are known as the Twelve Steps, all of which are spiritual in content. Every alcoholic is free to interpret each Step, and so one can expect a variety of thinking from alcoholics on A.A. However, the basic facts in the program must be accepted as spelled out to assure sobriety.

Regarding their program, the big A.A. book says, "Rarely have we seen a person fail who has thoroughly followed our path. Those who do not recover are people who cannot or will not completely

---

[3]*Ibid.*, pp. 63-64.
[4]*Alcoholics Anonymous* (A.A. World Services, Inc., N.Y.C., 1955), p. 13.

give themselves to this simple program, usually men and women who are constitutionally incapable of being honest with themselves. There are such unfortunates. They are not at fault; they seem to have been born that way. They are naturally incapable of grasping and developing a manner of living which demands rigorous honesty. Their chances are less than average. There are those, too, who suffer from grave emotional and mental disorders, but many of them do recover if they have the capacity to be honest."[5] The necessity of personal honesty must be emphasized as a basic requirement if the person is going to be able to be helped by A.A.

Speaking to alcoholics, they also say this, "At some of these [Steps] we balked. We thought we could find an easier, softer way. But we could not. With all the earnestness at our command, we beg of you to be fearless and thorough from the very start. Some of us have tried to hold on to our old ideas and the result was nil until we let go absolutely.

"Remember that we deal with alcohol—cunning, baffling, powerful! Without help it is too much for us. But there is One who has all power—that One is God. May you find Him now!

"Half measures availed us nothing. We stood at the turning point. We asked His protection and care with complete abandon."[6]

The following are the suggested Steps of recovery:

"1. We admitted we were powerless over alcohol—that our lives had become unmanageable.

"2. Came to believe that a Power greater than ourselves could restore us to sanity.

"3. Made a decision to turn our will and our lives over to the care of God *as we understood Him.*

"4. Made a searching and fearless moral inventory of ourselves.

"5. Admitted to God, to ourselves, and to another human being the exact nature of our wrongs.

[5]*Ibid.,* p. 58.
[6]*Ibid.,* pp. 58-59.

"6. Were entirely ready to have God remove all our defects of character.

"7. Humbly asked Him to remove our shortcomings.

"8. Made a list of all persons we had harmed, and became willing to make amends to them all.

"9. Made direct amends to such people whenever possible, except when to do so would injure them or others.

"10. Continued to take personal inventory and when we were wrong promptly admitted it.

"11. Sought through prayer and meditation to improve our conscious contact with God, *as we understood Him,* praying only for knowledge of His will for us and the power to carry that out.

"12. Having had a spiritual awakening as the result of these steps, we tried to carry this message to alcoholics, and to practice these principles in all affairs."

The Twelve Steps were the result of some heated discussion. Prior to the formulation of these Steps, those who were members of what is now A.A. were sharing with other alcoholics the six suggestions that Ebby gave to Bill. This group, however, had rejected other ideas and attitudes of the Oxford Group from which these six steps came. Among those rejected were any that would involve theological controversy.

Bill felt that the six steps might have to be broken into more steps in order to make the program more explicit and that there would not be a "single loophole through which the rationalizing alcoholic could wiggle out."[7] When he finished his first draft of rewriting the steps, he had twelve. Two friends who saw the new version reacted violently at first: "Why 12 steps? You've got too much God in these steps; you will scare the people away. What do you mean by getting these drunks down on their knees when they ask to have all their shortcomings removed? Who wants all their shortcomings

---

[7] *Alcoholics Anonymous Comes of Age,* p. 161.

removed, anyhow?" After some reflection, they admitted, "Well, some of this stuff does sound pretty good after all," but advised him, "Bill, you've got to tone it down. It's too stiff. The average alcoholic won't buy it the way it stands."[8]

There were others who liked and expressed their approval of the Twelve Steps. One recovered alcoholic, an Episcopalian minister's son from Maryland, "thought the book ought to be Christian in the doctrinal sense of the word and that it should say so."[9] He was also in favor of using biblical terms and expressions to make this clear. Another fellow was even more emphatic about this.

Some who opposed this "had no objection to the use of the word 'God' throughout the book, but they were dead set against any other theological proposition. They would have nothing to do with doctrinal issues. Spirituality, yes. But religion, no—positively no."[10] Agreement in theology would be impossible.

The atheists and agnostics at first "wanted the word 'God' deleted from the book entirely. They wanted a 'psychological book' which would lure the alcoholic in. Once in, the prospect could take God or leave him alone as he wished. To the rest of us this was a shocking proposal, but happily we listened and eventually learned something of great value."[11]

Although Bill resisted strenuously any change in the Twelve Steps, there finally was a compromise. They decided to describe God as "a Power greater than ourselves," and in Steps 3 and 11 they inserted the words, "God as we understood Him." "On our knees" was eliminated from Step 7. Regarding these changes Bill says, "Such were the final concessions to those of little or no faith; this was the great contribution of our atheists and agnostics. They had widened our gateway so that all who suffer might pass through, regardless of their belief or lack of belief. God was certainly there in our steps, but He was now expressed in terms that anybody—

---

[8]*Ibid.*, p. 162.
[9]*Ibid.*, p. 162.
[10]*Ibid.*, p. 162.
[11]*Ibid.*, p. 163

anybody at all—could accept and try. Countless A.A.'s have since testified that without this great evidence of liberality they never could have set foot on any path of spiritual progress or even approached us in the first place."[12]

This apparent "watering down" of God in their program may initially cause some pastors difficulty. But actually the more time a person spends with alcoholics and the more time he studies and experiences A.A., the more he is amazed at the content and arrangement of the Twelve Steps together with the careful excellent choice of key words. They truly bear the "marks of inspiration." Important also is the realization that A.A. is not and does not claim to be a church or a religion. This is not another "way of salvation" that is being offered to people. Their fellowship does not exist to meet this greatest need of man. This need is to be met in the fellowship of the church, to which God has entrusted the Word and the Sacraments. A.A. is in existence to help alcoholics attain sobriety and to help bring about changes within alcoholics to assure continued sobriety. It is a "way of salvation" from alcoholism. They have experienced and believe that there is a valid spiritual awakening, not necessarily Christian, in which alcoholics receive from God what they need to stay sober.

A.A. does not claim that it is the only way of recovery and hope for the alcoholic. The recovery of an alcoholic through what is thought to be a Christian conversion experience, for instance, they would not dispute. Members of the fellowship simply share with other alcoholics what proved to be the way of recovery for them. And this happens to be the way of recovery that reaches and helps the largest number of alcoholics.

Basically, "the great fact is just this and nothing less: That we have had deep and effective spiritual experiences which have revolutionized our whole attitude toward life, toward our fellows and toward God's universe. The central fact of our lives today is the absolute certainty that our Creator has entered into our hearts and lives

---

[12]*Ibid.*, p. 167.

in a way which is indeed miraculous. He has commenced to accomplish those things for us which we could never do ourselves."[13]

The first step is surrender to the reality of powerlessness over alcohol and of life being unmanageable. There is no better word to describe the nature of alcoholism and the dilemma of the alcoholic than the word "powerlessness." In this sense it is a powerful word. The alcoholic has to quit fighting because he is already defeated. As long as he continues to fight this reality, either in trying to quit or control his drinking, or simply by the slightest unconscious reservation about the reality of actual powerlessness, he continues to go down into defeat.

If we know ourselves at all, we know how difficult it is to accept the reality of our own powerlessness. The resistance within us is tremendous. So strong is this resistance that many times the only way we come to such acceptance is through severe crisis. This is one of the great potentials of alcoholism. It is the kind of problem that eventually drives the alcoholic into such acceptance if he is to go on living. Alcohol, as they say, "beats us to our knees."

So it is also with many inner conflicts and other problems. We are powerless. We need the help of others. We need to experience God's strength perfected in our weakness. Nevertheless, we seek to avoid, escape, deny the reality of our need. We even tend to consider admitting weakness a sign of weakness. The "real man" doesn't admit or accept the fact that he is defeated and needs help. But this is distortion because it is not weakness to accept the reality of weakness. Such acceptance is a responsible action. The alcoholic who surrenders to this reality experiences in his relationship to God and to people strength for his weakness and goes from strength to strength in his sobriety.

Not only is there the natural resistance to such a reality, but the alcoholic has intensified the resistance by telling others that he can handle his drinking. To have battled for years to "prove that he could" and then finally admit his powerlessness is as far from easy

---

[13] *Alcoholics Anonymous*, p. 25.

as anything can be. Not only that, but to realize and accept that this means no alcohol, which he drinks compulsively and which has been so tremendously important in his life, is difficult beyond the non-alcoholic's comprehension. This is one reason that A.A. doesn't put the emphasis on "the rest of your life" but just on "today."

Such surrender is one of the great hidden potential blessings of suffering. Fortunate is the person whose problems get him into trouble and anguish serious enough to bring him to surrender, and from which he turns to God in faith and commitment to learn that the Father is waiting with mercy and strength sufficient. At this point the great tragedy is not alcoholism but rather the alcoholic driven to the necessity of this experience and still ending up with something superficial. The vital experience of life which can come out of alcoholism is missed and filled with shallowness. But with the deep surrender process the door is opened for God, usually through others, to perform the wonders of his grace, in the life of a person who is ready to function as a responsible human being.

When surrender takes place, it is more than surrender to the reality of powerlessness over alcohol. Dr. Harry Tiebout states that "at the start of life the psyche: (1) assumes its own omnipotence, (2) cannot accept frustrations, (3) functions at a tempo allegretto with a good deal of staccato and vivace thrown in."[14] Remembering what has already been said about our "being by nature sinful" we see that what Dr. Tiebout says exists "at the start of life" is quite identical to the theological doctrine of original sin.

Man comes into this world with a sense of omnipotence. It is man's nature to assume from the start that he is the Omnipotent one who neither can nor wants to let God be God, neither can nor wants to be simply a created person. Divine afflatus exists in all men, lurking sometimes beneath a cloak of inferiority.

We here quote Dr. Tiebout at length because we feel that what he says will be very meaningful to pastors, not only in understanding

---

[14]Harry S. Tiebout, "The Ego Factors in Surrender in Alcoholism," reprint from *Quarterly Journal of Studies on Alcohol*, Vol. 15, pp. 610-621, December, 1954, p. 612.

the alcoholic and the surrender phenomenon, but also because of the interesting parallels here to the Christian doctrine of man.

"Now the question is, 'If this infantile psyche persists into adult life, how will its presence be manifested?'

"In general, when infantile traits continue into adulthood, the person is spoken of as immature, a label often applied with little comprehension of the reason for accuracy. It is necessary to link these three traits from the original psyche. If this is done, not only will the correctness of the appellation 'immature' be apparent, but moreover, a feeling for the nature of the unconscious underpinnings of the Ego will have been created.

"Two steps can aid in recognizing the relationship between immaturity and a continuance of the infantile elements. The first is, by an act of imagination, to set these original traits into an adult unconscious. The validity of this procedure is founded upon modern knowledge of the nature of the forces operating in the unconscious of people of mature ego. The second step is to estimate the effect that the prolongation of these infantile qualities will have upon the adult individual.

"This attempt should not strain the imagination severely. Take, for instance, the third of the qualities common to the original psychic state, namely the tendency to act hurriedly. If that tendency prevails in the unconscious, what must the result be? The individual will certainly do everything in a hurry. He will think fast, talk fast and live fast, or he will spend an inordinate amount of time and energy holding his fast-driving proclivities in check.

"Often the net result will be an oscillation between periods of speeding ahead followed by periods during which the direction of the force is reversed, the brakes (superego) being applied in equally vigorous fashion. The parallel of this in the behavior of the alcoholic will not be lost on those who have had experience with this class of patients.

"Let us take the same trait of doing everything in a hurry and apply it to the word 'immature.' Few will deny that jumping at conclusions, doing things as speedily as possible, gives evidence of immaturity. It is youth that drives fast, feels fast, moves fast, acts hastily in most situations. There can be little question that one of the hallmarks of the immature is the proneness to be under inner pressure for accomplishment. Big plans, big schemes, big hopes abound, unfortunately not matched by an ability to produce. But the effect upon the adult of the persisting infantile quality to do everything in less than sufficient time can now be seen in a clearer light. The adult trait is surely a survival from the original psyche of the infant.

"The two other surviving qualities of the infantile psyche similarly contribute to the picture of immaturity and also, indirectly, help to clarify the nature of the Ego with a capital E. The first of these, the feeling of omnipotence, when carried over into adult life affects the individual in ways easily anticipated. Omnipotence is, of course, associated with royalty, if not divinity. The unconscious result of the persistence of this trait is that its bearer harbors a belief of his own special role and in his own exceptional rights. Such a person finds it well-nigh impossible to function happily on an ordinary level. Obsessed with divine afflatus, the thought of operating in the lowly and humble areas of life is most distressing to him. The very idea that such a place is all one is capable of occupying is in itself a blow to the Ego, which reacts with a sense of inferiority at its failure to fill a more distinguished position. Moreover, any success becomes merely Ego fodder, boosting the individual's rating of himself to increasingly unrealistic proportions as the king side eagerly drinks in this evidence of special worth.

"The ability to administer the affairs of state, both large and small, is taken for granted. The belief that he is a natural executive placed in the wrong job merely confirms his conviction that, at best, he is the victim of lack of appreciation, and at worst, of sabotage by jealous people who set up roadblocks to his progress. The world is inhabited by selfish people, intent only on their own advancement.

"The genesis of all this is beyond his perception. To tell him that his reactions spring from the demands of an inner unsatisfied king is to invite incredulity and disbelief, so far from the conscious mind are any such thoughts or feelings. People who openly continue to cling to their claims of divine prerogative usually end up in a world especially constructed for their care. In others, the omnipotence pressures are rather better buried. The individual may admit that, in many ways, he acts like a spoiled brat, but he is scarcely conscious of the extent of the tendency, nor how deeply rooted it may be. He, like most people, resolutely avoids a careful look because the recognition of any such inner attitudes is highly disturbing. The unconscious credence in one's special prerogatives savors too much of straight selfishness to be anything but unpleasant to contemplate.

"And so, for the most part, people remain happily ignorant of the unconscious drives which push them around. They may wonder why they tend to boil inside and wish they could free themselves from a constant sense of uneasiness and unsettlement. They may recognize that they seem jittery and easily excited, and long for the time when they can meet life more calmly and maturely; they may hate their tendency to become rattled. But their insight into the origin of all this is next to nothing if not a complete blank. The king lies deep below the surface, far out of sight.

"The last trait carried over from infancy is the inability to accept frustration. In an obvious sense this inability is another aspect of the king within, since one of the prerogatives of royalty is to proceed without interruption. For the king to wait is an affront to the royal rank, a slap at his majesty. The ramifications of this inability to endure frustration are so widespread, and the significance of much that occurs in the behavior of the alcoholic is so far-reaching, that it seems advisable to discuss this trait under a separate heading.

"As already indicated, on the surface the inability of the king to accept frustration is absolutely logical. The wish of the king is the law of the land, and especially in the land of infancy. Any frustration is clearly a direct threat to the status of his majesty, whose whole being is challenged by the untoward interruption.

"Even more significant is another aspect of this inner imperiousness. Behind it lies the assumption that the individual should not be stopped. Again, this is logical if one considers how an absolute monarch operates. He simply does not expect to be stopped; as he wills, so will he do. This trait, persisting in the unconscious, furnishes a constant pressure driving the individual forward. It says, in essence, 'I am unstoppable!'

"The unconscious which cannot be stopped views life entirely from the angle of whether or not a stopping is likely, imminent, or not at all in the picture. When a stopping is likely, there is worry and perhaps depression. When it seems imminent, there is anxiety bordering on panic, and when the threat is removed, there is relief and gaiety. Health is equated with a feeling of buoyancy and smooth sailing ahead, a sense of 'I feel wonderful!' Sickness, contrariwise, means lacking vim, vigor and vitality, and is burdened with a sense of 'I'm not getting anywhere.' The need to 'get somewhere,' to 'be on the go,' and the consequent suffering from eternal restlessness, is still another direct effect of an inner inability to be stopped or, expressed otherwise, to accept the fact that one is limited. The king not only cannot accept the normal frustrations of life, but because of his inordinate driving ahead, is constantly creating unnecessary roadblocks by virtue of his own insistence on barging ahead, thus causing added trouble for himself.

"Of course, on some occasions, the king gets stopped and stopped totally. Illness, arrest, sometimes the rules and regulations of life, will halt him. Then he marks time, complies if need be, waiting for the return of freedom, which he celebrates in the time-honored fashion if he is an alcoholic: he gets drunk, initiating a phase when there is no stopping him.

"The immaturity of such a person is readily evident. He is impatient of delay, can never let matters evolve; he must have a blueprint to follow outlining clearly a path through the jungle of life. The wisdom of the ages is merely shackling tradition which should make way for the freshness, the insouciance of youth. The value of staying where one is and working out one's destiny in the here and now is not suspected. The 24-hour principle would be confining for one whose inner life brooks no confinement. The unstoppable person seeks life, fun, adventure, excitement, and discovers he is on a perpetual whirligig which carries him continuously ahead—but, of course, in a circle. The unstoppable person has no time for growth. He must always inwardly feel immature.

"This, then, is how the carry-over of infantile traits affects the adult so encumbered. He is possessed by an inner king who not only must do things in a hurry, but has no capacity for taking frustration in stride. He seeks a life which will not stop him and finds himself in a ceaseless rat race.

"All this is part and parcel of the big Ego. The individual has no choice. He cannot select one characteristic and hang on to that, shedding other more obviously undesirable traits. It is all or nothing. For example, the driving person usually has plenty of energy, sparkle, vivacity. He stands out as a most attractive human being. Clinging to that quality, however, merely insures the continuance of excessive drive and Ego, with all the pains attendant upon a life based on those qualities. The sacrifice of the Ego elements must be total or they will soon regain their ascendancy.

"Those who view the prospect of life without abundant drive as unutterably dull and boring should examine the life of members of Alcoholics Anonymous who have truly adopted the A.A. program. They will see people who have been stopped and who, therefore, do not have to go anywhere—but people who are learning, for the first time in their lives, to live. They are neither dull nor wishy-washy. Quite the contrary, they are alive and interested in the realities about them. They see things in the large, are tolerant, open-minded, not close-mindedly bulling ahead. They are receptive to the wonders in the world about them, including the presence of a Deity who makes all this possible. They are the ones who are really living. The attainment of such a way of life is no mean accomplishment.

"Preliminary to this discussion the conclusion was offered that the Ego was a residual of the initial feeling life of the infant. It should be evident that the immaturity characteristically found in the make-up of the alcoholic is a persistence of the original state of the child. In connection with the description of the manifestations which denote a large and active Ego, it should be recalled that the presence in the unconscious of such Ego forces may be quite out of reach of conscious observation. Only through the acting and feeling of the individual can their existence be suspected.

"Now the answer to the first question raised herein, namely, what part of the alcoholic must surrender, is obvious: it is the Ego elements.

"Life without Ego is no new conception. Two thousand years ago, Christ preached the necessity of losing one's life in order to find it again. He did not say Ego, but that was what he had in mind. The analysts of our time recognize the same truth; they talk also about ego reduction. Freud saw therapy as a running battle between the original narcissism of the infant (his term of Ego) and the therapist whose task it was to reduce that original state to more manageable proportions. Since Freud could not conceive of life without some measure of Ego, he never resolved the riddle of how contentment is achieved; for him man to the end was doomed to strife and unhappiness, his dearest desires sure to be frustrated by an unfriendly world.

"In his studies on the addictions, Rado more explicitly asserts that the Ego must be reduced. He first portrays the Ego as follows: 'Once it was a baby, radiant with self-esteem, full of belief in the omnipotence of its wishes, of its thoughts, gestures and words.' Then, on the process of Ego-reduction: 'But the child's megalomania melted away under the inexorable pressure of experience. Its sense of its own sovereignty had to make room for a more modest self-evaluation. This process, first described by Freud, may be designated the reduction in size of the original ego; it is a painful procedure and one that is possibly never completely carried out.'

"Like Freud, Rado thinks only in terms of reduction; the need for the complete elimination of Ego is a stand which they cannot bring themselves to assume. Hence they unwittingly advocate the retention of some infantile traits, with no clear awareness that trading with the devil, the Ego, no matter how carefully safeguarded, merely keeps him alive and likely at any occasion to erupt full force into action. There can be no successful compromise with Ego, a fact not sufficiently appreciated by many, if not most, therapists.

"Thus the dilemma encountered in ego-reduction would be best resolved by recognizing that the old Ego must go and a new one take its place. Then no issue would arise about how much of the earliest elements may be retained. The answer, theoretically, is none. Actually the total banishment of the initial state is difficult to achieve. Man can only grow in the direction of its complete elimination. Its final expulsion is a goal which can only be hoped for."[15]

These Ego elements are involved in surrender. Christ has said that a man must lose his life to find it. If a man wants to hang on to the infantile qualities described by Tiebout, he will lose his life. If he is willing to let go of these qualities, he will find life.

Not until this takes place in the whole man, conscious and unconscious, is there surrender. "One fact must be kept in mind, namely, the need to distinguish between submission and surrender. In submission, an individual accepts reality consciously but not unconsciously. He accepts as a practical fact that he cannot at the moment conquer reality, but lurking in his unconscious is the feeling, there'll come the day—which implies no real acceptance and demonstrates conclusively that the struggle is still going on. With submission, which at best is a superficial yielding, tension continues. When, on the other hand, the ability to accept reality functions on the unconscious level, there is no residual battle and relaxation ensues with freedom from strain and conflict."[16]

---

[15]*Ibid.*, pp. 612-618.

[16]Harry S. Tiebout, "Surrender Versus Compliance in Therapy, with Special Reference to Alcoholism," reprint from *Quarterly Journal of Studies on Alcohol*, Vol. 14, No. 1, pp. 58-68, March 1953, p. 59.

"There is a string of words which describe half-hearted acceptance: submission, resignation, yielding, compliance, acknowledgment, concession, and so forth. With each of these words there is a feeling of reservation, a tug in the direction of non-acceptance."[17] Surrender produces wholehearted acceptance.

A classic example of half-hearted or conscious acceptance only is the alcoholic who, after a severe binge, was in real trouble. His wife was talking about divorce and his job was in jeopardy. With this were his feelings of powerlessness, guilt, remorse, and self-hatred. He consciously felt and accepted that he needed help. A few days later, however, he was quite a different person. Now he was sure that he could handle things by himself and shortly proceeded to prove it by going on another binge. The Ego on the conscious level was for a while in a state of acceptance, but the unconscious Ego was not. Once the unconscious had time to assert itself, the apparent acceptance disappeared and he was once again the omnipotent one. Because the unconscious did not accept reality there never was surrender, only submission which for a while looked like surrender. Anyone who has worked with alcoholics has seen this phenomenon over and over again.

In another article[18] Dr. Tiebout includes the feeling states a woman alcoholic listed in regard to how she felt before and after surrender:

Before I felt ...	After I feel ...	
unstable	at peace	
tense	safe	
nervous	composed	
afraid	relaxed	I have learned the
guilty	contented	meaning of humility
ashamed	thankful	and meditation
pushed	cleansed	
incapable	sane	
uncertain	receptive	
unworthy	prayerful	
dismayed		

[17]*Ibid.*, p. 61.
[18]Harry S. Tiebout, "Alcoholics Anonymous—An Experiment of Nature," reprint from *Quarterly Journal of Studies on Alcohol*, Vol. 22, No. 1, pp. 52-68, March 1961.

When there is wholehearted surrender, the whole person, conscious and unconscious, has quit fighting, quit resisting reality, given in, accepted defeat and need for help. The omnipotent Ego has gone, and with this comes humility. However, Tiebout clearly points out, as does Christian doctrine, that the Ego never assumes that it should be stopped and should die, or that this can happen. On any given day it is a powerful enemy that can take control. This points up the significance of the 24-hour program in A.A. The alcoholic needs to begin each day in surrender. (Some of the evidences of surrender in alcoholics will be described in another section.)

Here is a paradox basic to Christian truth, witnessed by a psychiatrist as reality in A.A.: in surrender we find strength as God's strength is perfected in our weakness. This is not giving up. This is giving in, accepting the reality of powerlessness, of our creaturehood, of our imperfection. As long as the alcoholic is fighting this reality, either consciously or unconsciously, he continues to drink and when sober has severe inner tension. When he gives in, quits fighting this reality, surrenders, he is able to receive strength sufficient for sobriety and the tension subsides.

One final quote now from Tiebout. "With respect to the act of surrender, let me emphasize this point—it is an unconscious event, not willed by the patient even if he should desire to do so."[19] Is not this observation by this psychiatrist strikingly parallel to what the Scriptures call grace?

Before we leave Step 1, we take special notice that the last part of the Step reads " . . . that our lives had become unmanageable." Many alcoholics, as well as other people, who read or hear Step 1 miss this. Sometimes in working with an alcoholic we get the definite feeling that he is ready to accept his powerlessness over alcohol, but without knowing it, is still hung up on accepting the fact that his life has become unmanageable. This raises an interesting question. Is it generally rougher for an alcoholic to accept that his life has

---

[19]Harry S. Tiebout, "The Act of Surrender in the Therapeutic Process," National Council on Alcoholism, Inc., p. 3.

become unmanageable than to accept that he has become powerless over alcohol? Is that a bigger threat than the alcoholism? It could be. In terms of surrender it could mean the difference between surrendering to one's powerlessness and surrendering one's life.

When an alcoholic has surrendered to the reality of powerlessness and an unmanageable life, naturally he is in need of coming to believe in a power greater than *himself*—not just his powerlessness over alcohol. This is Step 2 in A.A.

A.A. in sound judgment, not being a church or a religion, leaves the theological formulation to the church and the individual. Reference has been made to the possibility that the term "higher power" may cause some pastors difficulty because of its vagueness. But we need to recognize, first of all, that God does not necessitate faith in Jesus Christ as Lord and Savior before he will help a person who, in a state of surrender, is seeking help for a problem like this. Secondly, the term "higher power" does not limit God in helping. Most agnostic alcoholics who in the beginning have difficulty even with "higher power" come to believe that the "higher power" is God if they continue to live the Twelve Steps.

It is also a fact that there are surrendered alcoholics who aren't yet ready for a more clear and definite concept of God. If we rush in too fast here with a specific concept of God, we may well close the door on people who are ready for the help God can give them. A.A. in this Step presents to the alcoholic the need for faith in a higher power. And does it in a way that enables them to meet the alcoholic with this truth right where he is at this point in his life. It is also true that some alcoholics may move too quickly, emotionally, superficially, at this point and end up on a "religious binge," which, like alcohol, becomes an "escape from" instead of the "way through" their problem. So A.A. simply holds this out as a necessary step and lets the alcoholic pick it up to interpret as he will.

Most important initially is the fact that the alcoholic is confronted with the reality of a "power greater" than *himself*. That there could *really* be such a power has never *really* entered his mind. He may have verbally many times even indicated his belief in God, but subtly he has never *really* believed that there is a power greater than *himself*. Once he *really* believes this, the door is open for him to become aware of God as the ultimate source of his help.

Having come to believe, which denotes a process experience, that God could restore him to sanity, the alcoholic must next make a decision to turn his will over to the care of God as he understands him. Theologically, this is part of the content and evidence of faith, but A.A. spells it out in a separate step. Surrender and faith involve movement that is commitment of life to God. And in this step we see that such movement is not just a matter of determination but a matter of willingness. Here, too, we begin to see the necessity for the alcoholic to face up to the fact that he is a responsible person who must assume responsibility for his problem and for doing what he needs to do in order to recover.

Sometimes an alcoholic, in talking with the pastor, will want to know how he goes about making this decision, what will happen when he does, and how he will know if he has. This can often be an indication that he isn't really ready yet. Very seldom does the surrendered alcoholic ask such questions. Rather he is aware of changes taking place which are an evidence of such commitment. If such questions are asked, we may feel constrained to "tell him" what we think are the answers. We should avoid this. It may be better to say that if this is something he wants and is ready for, it will come, and when it happens he will know it's happening. This leaves it where it belongs—with him and God. Beneath such questions could also be hidden the fear that this may cost him too much of himself, or the desire that all of a sudden all his problems will be solved, or even the unconscious desire to leave the door open for another drinking bout by being able to say, "I did what you said, but it didn't work."

An illustration of what happened in the third step is found in the case of an alcoholic who expressed concern that, although raised in a Christian home, he couldn't pray. There seemed to be a block between him and God. In essence he was asking, "How do I commit my life to the care of God?" The counselor stated that if he really was ready for Step 3 to take on reality in his life, this would happen. Some time later, in meeting with the alcoholic, the counselor could immediately see that something had happened. The anxious, tense expression was gone from the alcoholic's face. At this time he revealed that he was addicted not only to alcohol but also to gambling. In fact, he initially started drinking excessively to handle guilt from his gambling addiction. For a while he was ready to let God help him with his drinking but not with his gambling. When, in the solitary confines of his room, he surrendered to the reality of his powerlessness and need for help for his gambling addiction as well, the block was removed and he was ready to commit his whole self to the care of God.

In A.A. the words "as we understood Him" in Step 3 are italicized. With a distorted concept of God that makes him unthinkable or out of reach, it is often important for the alcoholic to see these words which hopefully will at least keep his mind open. At this point on the road to recovery such openness is an absolute essential.

Following this comes the necessity of taking "a searching and fearless moral inventory of himself." Two of the alcoholic's greatest problems are dishonesty with himself and guilt. The words "searching" and "fearless" are therefore chosen with real wisdom. It doesn't take fortitude for us to see and criticize the sins and weaknesses of others. This we do automatically. But it does take fearlessness to take a searching look at "me." The inventory is not just a matter of the alcoholic examining his drinking behavior. It is this, but more than this, it is an effort to honestly search out his selfishness, dishonest thinking, pride, resentments, fear, lust, impatience, envy, procrastination, and self-pity. These are common to man. For the alcoholic they spell "uncontrolled drinking." Crucial here for the alcoholic, as a clergyman friend who is in A.A. pointed out, is the realization and acceptance that all of this is not "just something about myself," but that "this is me." This is a basic part of the reality "within myself." It is necessary not only to face honestly what there is of this within himself, but also the positive aspects of his person that he may be enabled by God's grace to overcome and grow in the fruits of the Spirit.

When this step has been completed the alcoholic needs to "admit to God, himself and another human being the exact nature of his wrongs." Tournier, in his book *The Meaning of Persons,* says, "We become fully conscious only of what we are able to express to someone else."[20] Not until the alcoholic verbally communicates his inventory to another human being is he able to experience the "release" that A.A. talks about and know the importance of this step in his recovery. (Because of the vital significance of Steps 4 and 5 for the alcoholic and as a counseling situation for the pastor who may be the "other human being," they are dealt with more fully in another section.)

Many times an alcoholic coming off a binge has prayed that God would help him and promised "in the bargain" that "it would never happen again." The recovered alcoholic knows that such a prayer was not sincere. He was at the time only wanting to get out of the trouble he was in. He was not ready to surrender in his powerlessness and to look honestly at himself that he might receive the help he "really" needed. From such experience A.A. members have learned that before they ask they must become willing to receive from God that for which they pray.

Consequently, Step 6 reads, "Were entirely ready to have God remove all these defects of character," and then Step 7, "Humbly asked Him to remove our shortcomings." This is the step in which Bill had originally included the words "on his knees." A.A. recognizes how essential humility is in the recovery and continued sobriety of an alcoholic. It is a word that is frequently used in their meetings and in their talks.

One might almost feel that this should do it. But those who wrote these steps were led to know differently. The alcoholic needs more than this. Already, however, it is evident that it would be foolish to

---

[20]Tournier, *The Meaning of Persons,* Harper and Row, p. 22.

think that all of this can take on reality for the alcoholic over night. The man who said that not speed but thoroughness is important had good sense. On the other hand, procrastination, of which the alcoholic is expert, regarding any step can be very dangerous.

In the next step, particularly, the alcoholic must be on defense against rationalization and procrastination. He must now consider the people he has harmed: "Made a list of all persons we harmed and became willing to make amends to them all." Again he must swallow his pride, let go of any bitterness toward any and all that he has harmed, and "make direct amends to such people whenever possible, except when to do so would injure them or others." That word "direct" makes it tough. And although the alcoholic is doing this primarily for himself to safeguard his sobriety, he must here express real concern for others and continue to be careful not to hurt someone as he proceeds. Essential, also, is to put himself on the list and make amends with himself. He may have hurt a lot of people, but no one quite as much as he has hurt himself.

Sometimes the person with whom he seeks to make amends may be unreceptive, even rejecting. Still the alcoholic needs to fulfill his responsibility and in so doing, regardless of the reception, will resolve the problem. One alcoholic "skipped" someone in making amends because he felt it would be extremely difficult for him to confront that person. Later he saw the person on the street and experienced a tremendous anxiety reaction. He was told by some of his friends in A.A. that he simply had to make amends with that particular individual. With great difficulty he did, and although his effort was rejected, he felt better. Some months later the other person talked with him, restoring the relationship. The person whom the alcoholic has hurt may have forgotten all about it, but this is no reason for the alcoholic to fail to make amends. The alcoholic has not forgotten and therefore, for his own sake, must follow through.

In making amends the alcoholic not only helps himself to maintain sobriety, but also benefits through establishing new relationships with people he has hurt as well as a new relationship with himself.

This is the kind of procedure Jesus lays out for us when he says that before we bring our gift to the altar, we should go and be reconciled to our brother.

Because A.A. recognizes that at any time the Ego is a dangerous enemy and that, therefore, this is not just a "once for all" process, the next step deals with the importance of continuing to take a personal inventory and when wrong promptly admit it. That word "promptly" is particularly significant for the alcoholic in his sobriety. If it is not done this way, the wrong will fester within him and can easily start a serious infection that will some day break open in the form of a drinking spree. Alcoholics who have been dry for some time and then take to the bottle again are quite often "infected" in this way.

Coupled with this he is to "seek through prayer and meditation to improve his conscious contact with God as he understands Him, praying only for knowledge of His will for him and the power to carry that out." None of us stands still in our relationship with God. We either grow in this relationship or begin to lose that which already exists. The latter usually spells drinking for the alcoholic. From the church's point of view this step honestly followed should eventually lead the alcoholic into the Christian fellowship. How else can there be continued growth in his spiritual life?

When he wanted sobriety, he found he had to do more than pray. There was a place he needed to go and that place for him was A.A. He also discovered there was a fellowship which he needed to maintain sobriety—the fellowship of A.A. He further learned that there was a word he needed to hear for sobriety—the Twelve Steps of A.A. In the same way if his relationship with God is to deepen, if he wants knowledge of God's will, he must do more than pray. There is a place he needs to go and that place is the church to which God has entrusted his Word and Sacraments and in which he reveals himself and his will in Jesus Christ. There is another fellowship to which he must belong—the fellowship of believers. And there is a Word other and greater than the Twelve Steps which he needs to hear—the Word of God. Many recovered alcoholics, particularly among those who were raised in the church, come to this realization and a meaningful relationship within the fellowship of the church.

To keep anything good we have received, we must share it with others. So the alcoholic for his own sake and the sake of other alcoholics must pass this on. Step 12 reads, "Having had a spiritual awakening as the result of these steps, we tried to carry this message to alcoholics and practice these principles in all our affairs."

The alcoholic is aware that he must do the "Twelfth Step work," as they call it, in order to stay sober. There is a wholesome kind of self-concern here. But with this, the alcoholic also begins the process of living his life "outside of himself" in concern for others. He can share because of what he received and now has. This is the kind of sharing in which he will go out to his brother alcoholic, communicating in feeling and word the "good news" but without forcing anything upon him. He accepts the fact that what he has to share will only and can only be received by another when the other is ready to know and accept that which can set him free from the bondage of his alcoholism. He is the "symbol of hope" in flesh and blood.

A further look at these Twelve Steps reveals that the order in which they come is very significant. No step can ultimately take on reality without the preceding step. In A.A. we frequently hear about the "one stepper" or "one and twelfth stepper." These are people who supposedly have only taken Step 1 or Steps 1 and 12. That this is ineffective, actually an impossibility, is proved by the fact that these people generally continue to have trouble with drinking. Then, too, there are a number of people in A.A. who have never taken Steps 4 and 5. Until these steps are taken the remaining seven cannot be honestly taken.

To further point up how it is taken for granted in A.A. that these steps are and need to come in order, we quote from the big A.A. book a paragraph following the discussion on the fifth step. "Returning home we find a place where we can be quiet for an hour, carefully reviewing what we have done. We thank God from the bottom of our heart that we know Him better. Taking this book down from the shelf, we turn to the page which contains the Twelve Steps. Carefully reading the first five proposals, we ask if we have omitted anything, for we are building an arch through which we shall walk a free man at last. Is our work solid so far? Are the stones properly in place? Have we skimped on the cement put into the foundation? Have we tried to make mortar without sand?"[21]

Quite obviously, not all alcoholics in A.A. reflect all these spiritual realities in their lives. But someone has said that eventually they can smell the phonies in A.A.—there can seldom be continued sobriety where there is phoniness. However, we do see the phenomenon of an alcoholic who finds that his unhealthy Ego needs are being met in being an alcoholic in A.A., and with sufficient approbation he manages to stay sober without any real surrender and inner change.

It is vitally important for a pastor to get well acquainted with a few alcoholics whom he feels have and are experiencing the spiritual realities of A.A. Referrals to A.A. should be made through such a person so that the pastor knows the alcoholic will be exposed to "the real philosophy of A.A."

Incidentally, one of the rewards for the pastor can be his own spiritual enrichment in getting to know certain people in A.A. and occasionally attending their meetings.

A sometimes hidden and sometimes quite apparent danger in A.A. is that the alcoholic may end up finding his identity in being an alcoholic instead of finding it in being a person who is an alcoholic. He perceives himself as "being different and unique" from other human beings. The only meaningful identification he makes is with other alcoholics, and their conversation continuously centers around alcoholism. Necessary to the recovery and growth of the alcoholic is the capacity to enter into other meaningful personal relationships and activities.

There are too many alcoholics in congregations who never really

---

[21]*Alcoholics Anonymous*, p. 75.

become a part of the congregation, because their lives are so completely absorbed in A.A. and with other alcoholics. This is also often true for many in regard to their social life. Such a situation is understandable because of their common problem, and because they have had a unique experience that is found in a fellowship that is bound together by understanding, acceptance, and *self-honesty*. Seldom, yet today, would they find within any group, social or church, a similar fellowship. In most other groups, few have become aware of and shared their weaknesses with one another. There is too much mask wearing. The church needs to, and can, learn much from the nature of the A.A. fellowship.

Nevertheless, alcoholics need to become aware of the fact that although they have experienced a unique kind of fellowship, they were not created just for a fellowship with alcoholics. They are persons in whose lives the common human problem has found expression in alcoholism. Hopefully they can be helped to see the common human problem, not just the problem of alcoholism, and helped to find their way into the world of persons, not just the world of persons who are alcoholic, and into the community of the church, not just the community of alcoholics.

When an alcoholic is ready for help from A.A. he has a sponsor, another member of A.A., who acquaints him with A.A., helps answer questions, gives him support whenever needed, particularly in the beginning, continues to work with him in case of a "slip," and seeks to help whenever and wherever possible. The sponsor, it is hoped, does this in such a way that the newcomer knows that his sobriety and facing realities are primarily his own responsibility and that he needs to grow toward healthy dependence. If he is in a larger community where there are a number of A.A. members, he will join a particular squad that meets regularly each week. Smaller communities have only one group, one squad, of which he automatically becomes a member.

There are basically two kinds of meetings, the "open" and the "closed." Most groups have an open meeting regularly or occasionally to which the public is invited. Many times these meetings consist of alcoholics' telling their story and how they recovered in A.A. The closed meeting is self-explanatory. The subject may deal with one of the Twelve Steps, basic virtues, common defects, or specific problems common to alcoholics. This is the best kind of A.A. meeting. Some groups encourage the spouse of the alcoholic to attend the meetings, others are for members only. Members are free to say what they think and feel as they seek to help one another in their common problem.

Each meeting is opened with a moment of silent prayer, during which the members stand with heads bowed. The meeting is closed by praying the Lord's Prayer audibly and not in haste.

The pastor who becomes involved in meaningful relationship with alcoholics and is accepted by A.A. will be asked to speak at their meetings. Here the pastor should remember that he is asked to speak because he is a pastor. He should be able to speak in depth and with understanding on the spiritual truths of A.A. Sometimes a pastor, particularly in the smaller community, may be instrumental in getting an A.A. group started. They might even meet in his church. It is all-important that this doesn't become "his" group, but rather that he be a resource person as the alcoholics seek to establish and maintain "their" group.

A.A. is the most readily available help for most alcoholics. People who continue to work with alcoholics, whether they be pastors, psychiatrists, psychologists, or social workers, will usually come to realize and accept the fact that there must be direct treatment of the symptom (compulsive drinking). This is basic in the approach of A.A. Consequently, these people, while they continue to work with alcoholics, will frequently, at the appropriate time, refer them to A.A. for help to arrest the drinking. For professional people as well as for the alcoholics, A.A. is a godsend.

But A.A. alone is not enough for many alcoholics. And many in A.A. are still unaware of this. Too frequently the failure to recover in A.A. is attributed to the alcoholic's just "not being ready yet," when in some cases there may be a severe emotional disorder which also needs treatment. Therefore the "team approach" is essential. The professional people need A.A., but A.A. also needs the professionals. A.A. has become aware of and given expression to this need. "We need to be friends with our friends." It is regrettable that some A.A.'s and some professionals have the need to go it alone in helping alcoholics to recovery. One of the most interesting, enlightening, and rewarding aspects of the treatment of alcoholism is the inclusion of alcoholics who have recovered within A.A. as lay "therapists" on the treatment team.

APPENDIX

Some observations on the surrender phenomenon by a non-alcoholic pastor-friend in regard to his own life: It's taken me a long time to get the impact of this. I've tried too long to live without dying and as a result have lived without really living. This is not to say that self-awareness and honesty weren't there. I think they were. The more I saw, the more I feared the "letting go," the threat of non-being, a zero. A phony is better than a zero, I kept telling myself. One can get to the point of not daring the risk of faith—the faith that assures that "underneath are the everlasting arms." But until one takes the leap of faith, he will never know.

He may have all the concepts: acceptance, honesty, self-awareness, forgiveness, the love of God, Bible verses, as I had, but never feel any of these realities.

Maybe one of the reasons forgiveness was never *real* for me, real in terms of my feeling forgiven, lies in the area of my not forgiving myself—not forgiving myself for that which I have done, but also for what I am. The real dilemma was that I wanted love so badly, but never really experienced it. Feeling loved involved my seeing what there was to love in myself, and I saw nothing there. To really be loved by God or by other persons would mean that they had looked inside me—that they had seen me—that they knew. I could never let anyone do this, and therefore I never stepped out of my loneliness into meaningful relationship.

Those who said they loved me must not really have meant it. For me to be loved was to be loved unconditionally. I'd be loved if .... Those who said they loved me really didn't, I thought, because they never really knew me. I didn't, I couldn't, I wouldn't let them know me. "Like an infant he tries desperately to walk alone and erect. But his lack of self-confidence, his low level of self-regard, his painful sense of inadequacy, trips him up repeatedly into dependence he has so loudly renounced. His one hope of escape is a never-never land of omnipotence, where insecurity will be no more and where no one will reject. There will be at long last acceptance. There will be love. He does not know what is happening to him. He knows only pain and the desperate loneliness."[22]

Unlike the alcoholic, I did not find alcohol. That's the only difference. Omnipotence was achieved by being the best athlete, the best student, the greatest debater. I was applauded for my decision to enter the seminary. They did not know why I made the decision, but I did. Attainment was something I longed for, but attainment never satisfied. It involved perpetuating the image I had created for and about myself. It was so hard to maintain that image and yet force, or forces, compelled me to do it. I condemned the damn pietists and legalists who wouldn't let me be myself, but it was I who was the legalistic pietist.

Freedom to be the real "me" had to come from within myself. I could not surrender to my real self, to be what I knew I was. I had put on a "personage" (in Tournier's terms) to be what I wanted to be or to be what I thought I "ought" to be. Once I had done that, and who knows when I did that—I suspect it was something that developed throughout my life—it was hard to stay "up" there. I was always tense. People, including my wife, accepted this personage, but they weren't accepting me—because the real "me" was hiding.

The guilt for my dishonesty was always there. I preached "accep-

---

[22]Denis C. McGentry, *Inventory*, March, April 1959, p. 56.

tance" whenever I preached. "God accepts us as we are, allowing us to accept others *and ourselves* as they and we are." But how much of this preaching was an attempt to prepare my listeners to accept me *where* and *if* the real "me" would step outside of the clerics? Or how much was an attempt to convince myself that this is what God would do for me?

I knew this was why I preached this way. I knew I was a noisy gong and a clanging cymbal. I knew I had not *surrendered*. I was not ready to hit bottom even though I knew I was already at bottom. I was being called to be human, to be numbered among the transgressors. I was being called to "die" that I might live.

There were many things about myself that I had accepted (compliance not surrender). I could not do otherwise, but my resentment was always there. I "accepted" the fact that I was not the most intelligent, but I resented not being the most intelligent. I accepted my looks, but resented the fact that I wasn't good-looking. I accepted my poor health and physical disability, but deeply resented a God who could allow this to happen to me—of all people! My weaknesses, failures, and shortcomings were a constant embarrassment. "All fall short of the glory of God" . . . but not me!

I was hard on my wife and children when they embarrassed me by failing to live up to the image that surrounded me. Much of their "misbehavior" was simply my projected fears of being "exposed," and my "discipline" was retribution.

I always questioned the joy that some people said that they had. I questioned it because I hadn't found it myself. My problem lay in the fact that I felt I deserved the things that fell my way.

Maybe I haven't experienced surrender, and yet something has happened. I know not when or how it happened. I am experiencing some of the "after-effects" and yet there are areas in my life with which I am still struggling. I'm still resentful, bitter, and depressed about my physical disabilities. Daily pain and discomfort seem to nourish this resentment. For the time being, I have settled for something less than surrender in the area of my physical health. A degree of contentment and peace has come; for the time being, I've accepted my non-acceptance as a reality (if such is possible). Perhaps I'll never come to acceptance of this in my life, but in the meantime I'm asking that he will give me grace to live with it.

I'm quite sure I was confused when this surrender phenomenon began to make its inroads on my life. I equated surrender as giving up instead of giving in. It has been helpful to see and feel the difference.

I don't know when it happened or how. But something happened. I feel differently now about myself, others, and God. Before I was always "tooting a horn" and wishing that people would wake up and see me, especially my bishop and the church. Now I don't need to do that as much. There are more areas in my life where this phenomenon has yet to take place.

It used to be so easy to put the blame on someone else for the way I felt—my parents, my wife, my children, the church officials, or my congregation. Somewhere along the line came the realization that this can't go on, and yet it isn't easy to realize that I and only I am responsible for the way I feel.

From where I stand now, the surrender phenomenon is something that has happened and is happening, but it is something that also is yet to happen.

IV.

COUNSELING THE ALCOHOLICS

For many years now we have been calling certain people "alcoholics." We will continue to do this. And there isn't anything particularly bad about this unless—*unless* in calling them alcoholics we lose sight of the fact that they really are not alcoholics—they really are people, human beings—human beings who have the illness of alcoholism. Their identity, their name tag, is not "alcoholic." Their identity is "person," "human being," "Bob," "Ruth," "Jim," "Mary," "child of God." They are flesh of our flesh, bone of our bone, emotion of our emotion, spirit of our spirit. They are not "different people." They are not a "strange breed" of people. They are not more sinful than other people. They are people.

There are variations and degrees of physical, mental, emotional, social, and spiritual ill health among people who have the illness of alcoholism. Spiritually, alcoholics are sick, as all people are to some degree—spiritually sick. They are in need of the grace of God, but they are not in need of *more* of the grace of God than the rest of us.

Now all of this is terribly important. It is terribly important because this puts "them" and "us" in the same place, on the same level, with the same identity. And both "they" and "we" have a difficult time coming to realize, understand, and accept this very simple truth. There is the hidden, subtle desire to be someone "better" or "different" than other people. One of the great hidden fears is the fear that one may discover that truly he is like other people. This can be very deflating to the big Ego, but it also opens the door to the possibility of intellectually, emotionally, and spiritually joining the human race.

Anyone who has this awareness or reality within himself has the most basic requirement toward effective counseling with alcoholics. If this is present, alcoholics will sense it, and if it isn't present, they will sense that too. Alcoholics are so expert at being phonies that they are experts at spotting a phony. This can be one of the most threatening aspects for a pastor in his initial counseling of alcoholics.

Such awareness, mutual identity, and acceptance is one of the most basic factors in the effectiveness of A.A. Their spiritual program of recovery is tremendous, but it would be empty and without power if it weren't for the nature of the relationships and fellowship in A.A.

All of this is important for another reason. When we realize that alcoholics are actually people, then we realize that they have the same tendency in their thinking and feeling reactions about themselves and their problem that other people do. They, as we have seen, rationalize, alibi, project, deny, lie, and procrastinate. They insist on proving that they don't have a problem, or if they do admit they have a problem, they insist that they can lick it by themselves. They feel inadequate, hostile, guilty, remorseful, resentful, and sorry for themselves. They want other people to feel sorry for them too, but like other people they will not readily admit they want other people to feel sorry for them too. They hate themselves for their behavior. They also have tremendous, oversized Egos that not only necessitate perfectionism and immediate satisfaction of their needs, but actually also necessitate that they be someone other than just another member of the human race. And who among us nonalcoholics is not aware of these realities in some degree within ourselves?

Alcoholics' thinking and feeling reactions are sometimes called "alcoholic thinking." It isn't really. It's "people thinking." Really it's par for the course for a person with this kind of problem to think and feel the way he does. So, all of this rationalization, denial, defensiveness, evasiveness, hostility, resentment, etc., shouldn't surprise us, threaten us, or cause us to be continually angry toward the alcoholic unless so much of this is simply a reflection of realities within ourselves that we are not aware of. It is understandable, and until something significant begins to happen inside the alcoholic in terms of awareness, understanding, and acceptance of the nature of alcoholism, that's the way he is going to be.

When we realize that alcoholics are people and how people who are trapped and in deep inner pain think, feel, and react, then we also understand that the alcoholic doesn't need moralizing. He doesn't need lecturing. He doesn't need someone trying to manipulate him into a certain way of thinking, believing, and behaving. He doesn't need someone feeling sorry for him. He doesn't need someone pampering him. He doesn't need someone overprotecting him.

He does need someone and a society who understands alcoholism. He does need someone who understands how he feels and cares about him and his feelings. He does need someone who can help him become aware of the possibility and nature of alcoholism. He does need someone who can communicate that there is hope and help.

He also needs someone who is free to let him go—who can love him enough to completely let him go to the bottom, like unto the love of the father in the story of the prodigal son. He does need someone who is free to let the problem prove itself to him. He does need someone who is free to let him experience the inner pain and natural results of his drinking without imposing other pain upon him. He does need someone who can let the problem be his problem and at the same time seek to motivate him to responsible action.

Imagine the surprise and how the alcoholic is caught off guard when this person turns out to be the pastor who, strangely enough in many cases, he felt would be the last person to be this kind of person.

What we are saying here is that although techniques in counseling are important and vary with each person, they are not primary. Primary is "who we are," how we perceive ourselves and the person who is the alcoholic on the emotional and spiritual levels of our being.

Most basic then is that which is essential to establishing meaningful relationship with the alcoholic. Where this is present, the rest will come with time and experience in an intuitive manner, and become a part of the counseling relationship as it uniquely fits in with our particular personality functioning. It is only through experience that a pastor can develop the necessary "feel" of the alcoholic's feelings and thinking. Some knowledge and understanding of this, however, can come through attending A.A. meetings, reading the literature, getting to know and spending time with recovering alcoholics in A.A., attending one of the one-week schools on alcohol studies, and if possible, the Rutgers Summer School of Alcohol Studies.

What we have said also applies to the Christian community. By its very nature and responsibility, the fellowship of the church should incarnately express to the alcoholic, inside and outside the church, this kind of awareness and love. By who he is and by verbal communication, the pastor will or will not communicate this in his relationships with the people in his congregation. It is hoped that the leaven will be there and begin to leaven the whole group so that alcoholics and their spouses will more readily seek help.

All of us have "success needs." If they are primary in our motivation to help the alcoholic, we are in trouble, and so is the alcoholic we are trying to help. Such a pastor will become too emotionally involved and his anxiety for the recovery of the alcoholic will be transferred to the alcoholic. He will easily become hostile towards the alcoholic, foster excessive dependency, and be unable to let the alcoholic carry the responsibility for his own recovery. Such a person the alcoholic can also readily use and manipulate, and may well delude himself into thinking that in the process he is actually seeking and getting help. The counseling relationship is essentially perceived and necessarily needs to be one in which there is the kind of meaningful relationship in which the counselor can be a channel of God's grace. It is part of the wisdom of God to use people as such a channel as Paul so clearly describes.

Christ is clothing himself in the human need of the alcoholic just as he is in all need. He is coming in this person and will perform the wonders of his grace in his way and in his time as the alcoholic hopefully reaches the point where he is openly ready to receive. Inherent in this is the freedom to let God be God so that we do not get in his way.

The alcoholic when first seen may be grandiose, hostile, submissive, and usually will minimize or deny his drinking problem. In the beginning the pastor should let him talk, stay close to his Ego, and reflect his feelings in an understanding, accepting way. If a continuing relationship does not come about after the first interview or two, the initial understanding and attitude will determine if the alcoholic will return at a later date when he feels more keenly the need for help.

Direct Treatment of the Immediate Problem

In the first stage of the counseling we concentrate on the compulsive drinking and on direct treatment of this symptom which has become an illness. We are not primarily concerned with any underlying problems which may or may not eventually become a part of the counseling or referral process. Sometimes there is immediate obvious indication of a severe underlying disorder which indicates referral as soon as possible. However, it is to be hoped that the pastor will not drop out of the picture when such a referral is made.

Here again we stress the fact that the compulsive drinking, which is in reality the symptom of unresolved estrangement, is the immediate problem. Not until the alcoholic comes to face the reality of his loss of control over alcohol is he apt to benefit from efforts to resolve any underlying conflicts. A basic dishonesty, rationalization, or as the A.A.'s call it, "stinking thinking" and defiance preserves the drinking of the alcoholic while protecting him from the truth. As long as his drinking or the desire to drink continues, this is present and blocks the probability for significant insight into himself and his other problems.

Certain alcoholics, in a state of submission, are able to gain some insight regarding their inner conflicts. Usually, however, this is only on the intellectual level, and they do not responsibly use this awareness until after the surrender phenomenon has taken place. Furthermore, when an alcoholic is ready for help, he usually isn't immediately concerned about why he started drinking or why he became an alcoholic. In fact, if this is his primary interest, he perhaps isn't ready yet to be responsible in accepting his loss of control over alcohol and is hoping to find an answer that will enable him to drink with control. Rather, if he is ready, he wants to know what he needs to do to keep from drinking. This is his immediate pressing problem.

Dr. Tiebout says this about direct treatment of the symptom: "With the acceptance of the validity of the direct approach, the treatment of the alcoholic individual takes on a new dimension. Instead of determining causes, the therapeutic aim is toward helping the patient to utilize available techniques, A.A., Antabuse, and/or psychiatry, to aid in his battle to stop drinking. The therapist, so to speak, has his prescription. His job is to sell it to the patient.

"At this point we run into a fundamental issue. Most patients take their doctor's prescription. Very few alcoholics respond that simply. As a result, the doctor has the task of inducing the patient to take the medicine offered; and it is here that we must consider the nature of the alcoholic, the individual who balks at taking the remedy suggested. This brings us to our second point, namely, the nature of the individual who so stubbornly refuses to stop drinking.

"More accurately, the topic of this section is the nature of the individual's reaction to direct treatment. The physician for the alcoholic, regardless of his personal inclinations or his theoretical convictions about the function of the therapist, is placed in the role of someone who is trying to stop the patient's drinking. And although the alcoholic may desperately want help consciously, this does not necessarily overcome his unconscious resistance to such authoritative handling. The therapist inevitably acts as a depriving person.

"To try to avoid that role is silly, misleading, and a very poor example. Silly because it denies the obvious, and misleading because it is attempting to sugar-coat an unpalatable truth. A poor example, because the therapist is denying reality-behavior at which the patient is already expert. Fundamental respect can never be established on such a false basis.

"As a consequence, the therapist must not fight the patient's identification of him as a depriving figure. There is no loophole from that position. The only hope is to help the patient learn to accept deprivation, and therefore reach a state in which, as a mature person, he will realize that all his wants and demands cannot be satisfied and that there are some things he cannot have.

"The therapist must not sidestep his depriving role; instead he must freely acknowledge it and let therapy begin right there. To do so clears the atmosphere and paves the way for establishing a sound working relationship."[1]

What applies to the physician, applies to the pastor. Some feel that the pastor cannot assume such a role, because from his very position as a pastor he will appear moralistic. This certainly will not be true if the relationship is based on real understanding and acceptance.

Dr. Bacon, Director of the Center on Alcohol Studies, formerly of Yale and now of Rutgers State University, uses the idea of direct treatment in his answer to the question of why psychiatrists haven't done better. "One answer to this would be that the psychiatrist, quite correctly, sees that this person has personality difficulties, and in some instances, they see a long lasting character neurosis, one that's been in the developmental stages for years, perhaps since the age of four or five. So the psychiatrist says that unless we get rid of this thing at the bottom, we are just playing games with the thing at the top.

"So the alcoholic comes into his office and the psychiatrist starts

---

[1] Harry M. Tiebout, "Direct Treatment of a Symptom," reprint from *Problems of Addiction and Habituation*, Greene and Stratton, Inc., 1958.

needling back into this, perhaps adolescent problem, and then back
to the seven or three-year-old period. The alcoholic looks at the psychiatrist and wonders, 'Which one of us is screwy?' Here he is: his
wife is going to toss him out on his ear, he can't hold food in his
stomach, his glasses are smashed, he has lost his papers, he is going to
lose his job. He has this horrible feeling of fear, of additional worry
about this alcohol business, and here this weird character is asking
him what dreams he had about his great-grandmother when he was
four years old.

"Yes it is [an exaggeration], but it is significant of a very important thing: the psychiatrist, very correctly, proceeds on the premise
that there were underlying difficulties much more significant than
the actual effect of the alcohol. And so they begin to talk about alcohol as a symptom; but I would suggest to you that, as the alcoholic
has gone through alcoholic experiences for many years, he is no
longer merely neurotic Type B or a neurotic Type C. He may once
have fitted such a label, but now he has added alcohol dependency
and has fused the two into something new. He has problems, de-
manding problems, problems that have gone so deeply into his in-
sides that this alcohol will trigger him off fifteen to twenty years
later, even if he never takes a drink in the interim. The alcohol
dependence is terribly important in itself. It is a new thing. It is
what we call 'alcoholism.' "[2]

On the same topic, Bailey and Fuchs say: "Many alcoholics, at the
time they initially turn for help, are not at all motivated to accept
psychotherapy, but rather tend to deny their emotional problems and
concentrate only on getting and staying sober. The helping person,
whose goals are orientated toward the resolution of underlying problems, may thus be failing to observe the cardinal principle of 'meeting the client where he is.' Effective treatment may thus constitute
welcome news to learn that many alcoholics can recover from their
alcoholism and lead productive and satisfying lives without any

---

[2]Selden D. Bacon, *The Facts About Alcoholism*, reprint from U.S. News and World
Report, p. 105, Oct. 2, 1953.

formal therapy aimed at the uncovering and resolution of unconscious emotional conflicts."[3]

To this we might add that for many alcoholics there is significant "uncovering and resolution" of inner conflicts within the A.A. fellowship, and that others who honestly seek help for their drinking do benefit greatly from counseling or psychotherapy.

Dr. Tiebout, in further discussing direct treatment, describes such treatment from clinical material and goes on to say: "First, the importance of timing cannot be overemphasized. The patient who reacted well to an active technique was ripe for the plucking. He wanted to quit and had been trying to for several years. He was a perfect candidate for the direct approach.

"Actually, he was at the end of a very long trail. It began with his drinking blithely and unconcernedly. It was nearing its conclusion hopefully with his earnest desire not to take the first drink. Space limitations prevent my identifying and discussing all the various sections of the trail. Suffice it to say that he could now seek help with no conscious reservations.

"Actually, such direct methods can be applied only when the patient is in a receptive frame of mind. A whole paper could be devoted to a discussion of how the patient's defenses must weaken so that he is willing and able to turn for help. To be direct where it is certain that such an approach will bounce off a shell-proof exterior is obviously bad timing. It wastes ammunition which could later be effective. Other measures must be used first in an effort to soften his defenses. The direct approach can be ventured only when the patient is sufficiently vulnerable to make its success likely.

"Secondly, what should be the doctor's attitude towards the patient's drinking during therapy? In the 'platform' placed before the patient, I included a 'wait and see plank.' This I did for three reasons. In the first place, I did not want to give the impression of acting

---

[3]Margaret B. Bailey and Estelle Fuchs, "Alcoholism and the Social Worker," *Social Work*, Journal of the National Association of Social Workers, Vol. 5, No. 4, October 1960, p. 19.

before I, too, was in possession of the facts about the drinking pattern. If it continued and caused difficulty, here was concrete evidence on which to base a decision about antabuse.

"A second reason for a tentative approach was the hope that the usual concept of the disciplinarian as dogmatic and arbitrary would be undercut if I adopted a less adamant program. If, later on, it became necessary to crack down, the patient would not be justified in claiming that the new tactics were evidence of a hopelessly closed mind toward drinking.

"One patient tried to punctuate that stratagem by ferreting out the reason for the delaying tactics and accusing me of waiting until he had hung himself. Since that was true I admitted the charge and went on from there. The focus was kept on the drinking problem; that he still had to face.

"The third reason for adopting a non-dogmatic policy was to place myself in the position of being able to discuss the problem of the drinking with the patient directly. Generally with such delaying tactics the patient makes an extra effort at control and as a rule succeeds for awhile, after which the condition usually takes its course and the patient gets drunk. At that point it is possible to review with him his hopes of controlling intake and his consequent disillusionment and renewed awareness of his drinking problem. In this manner, the patient's feeling of need for help is revived and motivation is thereby strengthened. Therapy can thus proceed on a firmer footing."[4]

Now we come to something about which many pastors have a serious question and which, from the point of view of counseling, can be easily misunderstood. The question is this, "Am I doing pastoral counseling when initially and essentially I just deal with the drinking?" And knowing the particular areas where many pastors doing counseling find themselves wondering about this, we are going to suggest that there is a big area in pastoral counseling in which the

---

[4]Tiebout, "Direct Treatment," pp. 23-24.

function is essentially judgmental and any verbal communication of the Gospel can be premature.

So often we hear that we are to be non-judgmental, and we lose sight of the fact that the word judgmental has two meanings. There is a judgmental attitude that is moralistic and rejecting, but there is also a judgmental attitude that is non-moralistic and non-rejecting. (When we use the term non-moralistic, we are not excluding morality. We perceive moralism and morality as quite different realities. Moralism is identified with rigidity, with a self-righteous condemning spirit, with being interested in someone because we not only want but actually "have to have" that person thinking and behaving according to our standards. In moralism there is not only rejection of immoral and irresponsible behavior, but essential rejection of the person.) The non-moralistic, non-rejecting judgmental attitude has the elements of understanding and acceptance, and moves in the direction of helping a person to greater self-awareness and greater honesty about himself and his condition, and his responsibility. It is basic in the process of confrontation.

DEF

This is evident in God's relationship with David and Job. It is evident in Christ's relationship with Mary, Nicodemus, Zacchaeus, the woman at the well, Peter, and Saul. Initially there was that which made essential and enabled the judgmental process in an accepting relationship. The scapegoats and defense mechanisms were maybe slowly, but surely, exposed, torn down, and removed, as in this relationship they were led to greater awareness about themselves, their condition, and responsibility for their feelings and behavior.

God in this sense was a "loving presence" but also a "convicting presence," a "disturbing presence," and we detect that within these people there was an awareness that if they didn't run away, things were never going to be the same again in terms of self-deception and self-awareness. They were caught up in a gracious judgmental, non-rejecting relationship in which there was a love that *would* let them go, but which they would not meaningfully experience until they honestly faced and accepted the truth about themselves and their condition.

We will consider only one of these people—Peter. Here was a man who felt he was somebody he really wasn't and who wanted to be someone he could never be—a human being essentially different from other human beings. Within him there was a tremendous sense of omnipotence and he had the unstable emotions of a child. Peter just didn't know Peter. He was always pretending, but chances are he didn't even know he was pretending. And this is the man Jesus called. But this was also a man in whom something had to happen before he could experience the love of Christ, his need for grace, and be set free to serve his Lord.

Peter, obviously, in his self-deception, perceived himself as being the greatest of the disciples. He made his proud boasts. For a while Jesus just let Peter be who he really was. But finally, when the time had come, Jesus just didn't let this pass anymore. He let Peter know that it wouldn't be like that at all, and then mentioned denial before the cock would crow. It is extremely significant that Christ inserted here the *crowing of the cock*. And because Peter was like us, what Jesus said possibly didn't penetrate his outer shell of defenses and self-deception. Or possibly it put a little crack in his outer shell and if for no longer, maybe for just a minute, Peter wondered what Jesus meant by what he said. However, if he did wonder at all about this, he probably quickly dismissed it and was more certain and determined that *he,* of all people, would never deny his Lord.

Jesus loved Peter enough to let him go and to let him learn—to allow the truth about Peter to reveal itself to him. This was a very judgmental process in his relationship with Peter.

And then it happened in the courtyard. Is this the same Peter? Obviously it is. But it isn't the same Peter that Peter previously perceived himself to be. Then the cock crowed. Peter remembered. The Lord wasn't standing there pointing his finger and saying, "I told you so." The cock crowed. That's all. And Peter was allowed to experience this truth about himself with all of its disillusionment. And somehow he also knew the Lord knew, not just now, but before. He was involved in a very judgmental relationship now with himself as well as with the Lord. It wasn't the Lord who caused him to boast, who sent him to the courtyard, who caused him to curse, swear, and deny. It was Peter.

And then they met again. Jesus looked at him. It wasn't a look of moralism and condemnation. It wasn't a look of "I told you so." It was a look that said, "Do you understand, Peter? Do you know what I was talking about?" He was allowed to experience the full reality and pain of it all. He went out and wept bitterly. But it was also a look that said, "Peter, I love you, and it is you, Peter, the man who has these realities within himself, that I want as my disciple; and for you, Peter, my grace is sufficient."

Now, because Peter better understood and accepted the real Peter and his real condition, the door was opened for him to experience the meaning, comfort, strength, and sufficiency of God's grace.

Then they met again. Peter was still Peter, but he was also different now. "Do you love me, Peter?" "Lord, you know." (What a switch that is.) "Feed my sheep." Through awareness of himself and his condition in a judgmental relationship, Peter came to surrender. The sense of omnipotence, the egocentricity, and all the rest was drastically affected. Peter was moved out of the center of his existence. Christ became the center of his existence, and in this Person and his love Peter found his identity as a child of God, and was set free from himself to be a disciple and grow in grace.

It is through such a judgmental process that a loving God leads us to that point where we can begin to experience both the need and the reality of his grace. Grace itself is inherent in this judgmental process. And it is an essential process that leads from knowledge about God's grace to the experience of his grace.

This is what we have in mind when we talk about judgmental counseling with a non-moralistic attitude. This is a relationship in which the person is enabled towards awareness of himself and his condition. This is a relationship in which cracks are put in the hard, outer defensive shell protecting the omnipotent, egocentric self. This is a relationship in which the person can fool himself, but hopefully not the counselor. This is a relationship in which the truth about himself and his condition is allowed to prove itself to him and sometimes is openly expressed to him. This is a relationship in which hopefully the counselor can let God be God and not get out in front of God in terms of where this person is and what this person needs at any given point.

With some the defenses go, and awareness of oneself and one's condition comes rather quickly. With others it may take months or even years. And, of course, for some it doesn't come at all. But neither of these is all-important from our point of view. All-important is whether or not we are able to have the kind of meaningful relationship with the alcoholic in which this process and event can take place.

Hopefully, it can now be seen that to be a pastor in a pastoral counseling relationship during a given period with a given person does not necessitate at all the verbal communication of the Gospel as is so often thought. There are times and processes in which this is both uncalled-for and premature, as Christ so clearly shows us. In fact, in so doing, we are often apt to close the door on a process that could eventually lead to a meaningful hearing and reception of the Gospel.

This "judgmental, non-moralistic" relationship and process is very much a part of pastoral counseling. We are making judgments about his condition and relating with him in such a way that he finds it increasingly necessary to make judgments about his condition. In essence and from a theological point of view, it is the process described by Dr. Tiebout and is essential in the direct treatment process with the alcoholic. It costs much more in terms of self, of concern, of caring, and of loving than readily and easily quoting Bible passages and proclaiming Christ to a person who is still in the clutches of omnipotence, egocentricity, defiance, and self-delusion, and *doesn't even know it*. He must come to know and accept the truth about himself and his condition before he can begin to hear, to know, and to receive the truth that can set him free.

The basic principle described by Tiebout and the reasons for it are valid and useful in our counseling relationship with the alcoholic. Obviously, there will be some kind of general conversation with the alcoholic before focusing in on his drinking. To deal directly with the drinking and keep the focus on the drinking is usually not difficult. Most people have been telling the alcoholic *how they feel* about his drinking and what he ought to do. And most of what they say feeds his drinking problem because it communicates moralistic judgment, condemnation, and rejection. He may expect the same from the pastor, but hopefully he has already sensed that the pastor will not attack him as others do.

The simple question, "How do *you* feel about your drinking?" can often have a very positive effect and lead even a hostile alcoholic to talk about his drinking. This may be the first time anyone has expressed interest in how he feels about his drinking. Besides an expression of genuine interest and concern, this is also staying close to his "Ego." He may well decide, "Here is someone different, someone interested in me and my feelings, someone who is for me, not against me." Even with such an approach, of course, there is the possibility that the alcoholic will reveal a "hard shell" of hostility and resentment and will refuse to talk about his drinking. If this is the case, the pastor must accept him where he is. "I get the feeling that you would rather not talk about your drinking." The pastor can then indicate that if in the future he comes to feel differently and would want to talk about his drinking or any other problems, the pastor would be glad to see him.

Usually, however, by reflecting back to this person what he is saying in an effort to make sure that nothing is misunderstood and by probing a little with a few questions, by staying close to his Ego, the pastor will be able to get him talking about his drinking.

We carry with us into the relationship two valid assumptions:

(1) that his drinking is bothering him; (2) that when he takes the first drink he seldom, if ever, consciously plans to get drunk, and thereby is evidencing *loss of control*. By keeping the focus on his drinking, we want these realities to find verbal expression in our relationship with him. When this happens, something significant in terms of understanding and awareness occurs in the relationship. At the same time the alcoholic's drinking is significantly spoiled, particularly since he will now be conscious of the *loss of control* factor in his future drinking.

The process may go something like this:

"You don't feel your drinking is a problem?"

"No, it's no problem. Sure, I drink too much sometimes. But my wife, she's always hollering about something. If it isn't my drinking, then it's something else."

"Do you feel that's why you drink the way you do sometimes?" (Notice how the focus is kept on the drinking and not transferred to the wife.)

"That's right."

"You get fed up and just decide to go out and get drunk."

"No, I don't decide to get drunk. I just start drinking and I end up drinking too much."

"You mean you don't plan to get drunk?"

"No, I don't plan to, it just happens."

We know that many people do decide and plan to get drunk. Alcoholics seldom do this consciously even when they buy a fifth of whiskey. To let himself consciously know that he is going to get drunk is insight—and insight is a luxury he can't afford when he is headed for a drunk. A classic example of this was in the television show on Playhouse 90, "Wine and Roses." Both husband and wife were alcoholics. They had tried to quit drinking and hadn't had a drink for some time. One day the husband took his father-in-law's truck, drove to town, and bought whiskey. Alone with his wife, he persuaded her that they ought to and could have just a little drink. As soon as she agreed, he pulled up his pants legs and there was a bottle attached to each leg. Later it was revealed that he had also planted one in the greenhouse. He had obviously planned to get drunk, but this plan had been completely blocked out from his consciousness so that consciously he was actually planning not to get drunk.

This may not be the time to share with the alcoholic the fact that the absence of conscious plan to get drunk is typical of alcoholics. But the matter could be explored further.

"Joe, if you don't plan to get drunk and end up getting drunk, how do you feel about it the next morning?"

"What do you mean?"

"Well, I would imagine you are kind of bewildered the next morning when you realize what happened even though you hadn't planned to get drunk."

"Ya, that's right."

"Your wife probably can't figure it out and is all shook up, but you can't figure it out either. Have you ever wondered why this happens the way it does?"

"What do you mean—that I drink?"

"No, that you end up getting drunk when you don't plan to drink that much."

Though obviously abbreviated and not completed, this simple conversation shows a process of exploration that keeps the focus on the drinking and stays close to the alcoholic's ego. This process works because we know that alcoholics are bothered and bewildered by their drinking. In most cases, such kind of communication is possible even with the openly hostile alcoholic, who certainly does not intend to talk about his drinking. The fact that he says even this much will indicate that something significant has happened.

A specific case history is appropriate here. An alcoholic's drinking had progressed to the point where his marriage was in real jeopardy. His wife sought help, and under pressure from her he came in. He was obviously hostile and evasive. In fact, he stated that he wasn't an alcoholic even though the pastor had not used the word.

Although he admitted that he sometimes drank too much, his drinking wasn't really the problem. He and his wife had some problems which, of course, were caused mainly by her. Things weren't good on the job. And besides this, he was naturally a very nervous kind of person.

When asked how he felt about his drinking, he said that he not only felt it was wrong to get drunk, but that he believed it was wrong to drink. (It is unusual for an alcoholic to make the latter statement.)

"You mean you feel it is wrong for anyone to drink?"

"Yes, I do."

"Why do you feel this way?"

"Because that's what I was taught. That's what the church teaches, isn't it?"

When the pastor said that some but not all churches and pastors teach this, the alcoholic tried to get the pastor to agree that it was wrong to drink and made the pastor feel that he wanted a good moral lecture on his drinking. When this didn't come, he was at a loss for what to think or how to feel.

As his drinking was explored apart from the moral aspects, it became obvious that he was an alcoholic. Although he didn't feel his drinking was a real problem, he did indicate that now he was going to "straighten out," quit drinking. When asked if he thought he could do this, he was sure that he could. The pastor pointed out that he might discover he couldn't. This, of course, made no sense to him, but the thought had at least been communicated. The pastor left him with the feeling that if he made it, fine. If he didn't, maybe he would want to talk about it some more.

His wife responded to the understanding and help she gained. Her husband previously had had her on the defensive. She had felt fearful and guilty, but in time this changed. She was no longer severely threatened by him and his drinking and was able to leave it with him. While she let him know that she felt he needed help, she also made clear that if he was going to drink, she couldn't keep him from drinking. This kind of attitude really threw him. He wanted to know what had happened to her and became exceedingly hostile toward the pastor. "If I ever do need help, I won't go to him."

Months passed in which his drinking rapidly worsened. He was charged three times with drunken driving and spent time in jail. Finally, the drunken driving charge in which he lost his license and his wife's threat to divorce him led to a phone call. He called the pastor. "I need help. I thought I could lick this thing, but it's got me licked. Could I see you?"

That sounded good, but the question remained whether this was submission or surrender. When he came in he was consciously sincere, but obviously there was no surrender. Now he was saying that he *really* had to quit and he was going to quit. When asked if he hadn't said this before he replied, "Yes, I have, but I never really meant it before." The pastor let him talk. He had told his boss one time that a number of the employees always missed work the day after payday. As soon as they had money they got drunk. The reason for this, according to him, was that they were alcoholics. A few minutes later he was telling about his last drunk. He had gotten some rent money, paid a few bills, and had some money left over. He got drunk.

"Whenever I have money like that, that's when I get drunk."

"You mean you're just like those fellows at work."

"That's right"—and his ready reply indicated that the truth of this admission didn't really penetrate his being.

The pastor accepted the fact that the alcoholic was consciously sincere both in his desire to quit drinking and in his belief that he could do it. After making clear that he did not question the alcoholic's sincerity, the pastor told him it was quite certain he would get drunk again. He explained that this would happen because when one has the illness of alcoholism he can't stay sober without outside help. The pastor took time to share some basic information about alcoholism.

The man continued to see the pastor, understanding that another drunk would be inescapable evidence of alcoholism. It was impossible to know, of course, whether another drunk would produce surrender or not.

This, then, is a case in which at the first interview the alcoholic was hostile and not at all ready to say he really had a drinking problem. By letting him talk, the pastor was able to do a little exploration. The moralism which the alcoholic had obviously expected did not materialize, and even though he shortly became very hostile towards the pastor, something had happened that established the kind of relationship which later resulted in his seeking out the pastor. He now knew that if he got drunk the pastor wasn't going to say, "I told you so," or even communicate this feeling. Rather they could talk about how he felt now that he put forth a sincere effort and still got drunk. This is a good example of what Tiebout calls submission in which there is conscious but no unconscious or whole-person surrender. Still intact in the unconscious is the omnipotent ego. Nevertheless, the counseling relationship was established and the "spoiling process" started.

Some time later this person was downtown with money in his pocket and, without consciously planning to get drunk, started drinking in the morning and naturally got drunk. Later he talked with the pastor and readily admitted that he couldn't figure it out. The door was now open for further talk about the possibility of alcoholism. The sickness aspect was emphasized because of his feeling that his drinking was only a moral problem. This time he was able to digest much information about alcoholism that previously didn't register. Another indication of progress toward surrender was his conscious awareness that, as he put it, he was "screwing himself" in his drinking. Primary in the picture before this were his resentments against others who were always giving him advice. Now he was evidencing some healthy conscious concern for himself.

At this point another statement by the pastor proved to be of real value. "You know, Bill," he said, "knowing you the way I do now, as a person who has some real moral convictions, I can understand your drinking and behavior—if you are an alcoholic. This all goes with the illness of alcoholism. But if you are not an alcoholic, knowing you the way I do, I can't figure out or understand your drinking and behavior. I can't imagine you deliberately planning to drink the way you do."

The important thing here is not whether this alcoholic ended up sober in A.A. or not. Significant is the fact that he developed a meaningful relationship with the pastor, and in this relationship made progress in becoming aware of the nature of alcoholism. Important, also, is the fact that the pastor did not allow the alcoholic to get him on the defensive. The alcoholic will often seek to do this and in so doing may become a threat to the pastor. This is an automatic procedure, and an extremely hostile alcoholic may be quite vicious in what he says. If the pastor is aware of this and expects it, through experience he ceases to be threatened and can learn different ways of handling such a situation so that what usually works for the alcoholic in his relationship with others doesn't work with the pastor. Instead, the pastor is able to get him to think and talk about his drinking, and in the process to put some cracks in the defensive shell.

Many of the alcoholics whom the pastor sees will not be so openly hostile. They will quite readily respond to a question such as, "How do you feel about your drinking?" with reactions like these:

"My wife thinks I drink too much, but I don't think I do. Oh, I get loaded once in awhile, but it's really not a problem."

"I know I drink too much, but I really don't have to drink."

"I know I drink too much sometimes, but I really like to drink."

"I know I drink too much sometimes, but I naturally am a nervous person and it calms my nerves."

Or they may appear to be ready for help by saying, "It's pretty obvious to me that drinking has got the best of me."

Any statement of this variety opens the door to the possibility of further exploration of the drinking. Although we use the word "interview," we are thinking essentially of just plain conversation about the drinking. There is no stereotype kind of interview or set of questions. The pastor simply seeks first to find out where the alcoholic is in his thinking about his problem and how much understanding he has of alcoholism. In hopes that some of the "feel" of the interview might be communicated, we can pursue a few of these typical comments a little further.

"I know I drink too much, but I don't have to drink."

"You feel that you do drink too much."

"Not all the time. Sometimes I do, but I don't have to."

"You mean you feel that you could control your drinking if you really tried."

"Sure. I know I can because I've done it many times. There have been a lot of times [that's probably an exaggeration] when I've just had a drink or two and that's all."

"So you don't get drunk every time you drink."

"No, no, of course not."

"When you do get drunk, do you plan to get drunk or how does it happen?"

"No, I don't plan to get drunk. I just am going to have a few with the fellows and you know how it goes. [That's one way of saying that he thinks even his getting drunk is "normal."] You get talking and the time goes by and you end up drinking quite a bit."

"You end up getting drunk even though you didn't plan to, is that it?"

"Ya, that's right."

"When you do end up getting drunk, missing supper, and not getting home until late, even though you didn't plan this, how does this make you feel?" (Now we are moving into an area that he keeps closely guarded. There is bewilderment, guilt, self-hatred about which he tells no one. He becomes angry and rationalizes and projects when his wife brings it up the next day.)

"I feel pretty cheap and low-down."

"So you don't like yourself after you've gotten drunk." (This is staying close to how he feels about himself rather than reflecting how others feel about him.)

"That's right."

"I suppose then you have tried to keep it from happening."

"That's right. And I know I can because I've done it. Just the other night I was with the fellows, had two drinks and went home."

"You feel you really could control your drinking if you tried."

"I know I could."

"Have you ever tried for any period of time?"

"You mean for a certain number of days or weeks? No, I've never tried that."

"Since this getting drunk bothers you, Jim, do you think you might be interested in seeing if you can control your drinking for a certain period of time?" (Here he may say he doesn't think that necessary or he may pursue the idea.)

"I don't know. I've never really thought about it too seriously. I have quit for periods of time, but I've never thought about controlling my drinking for a period of time."

"Would your wife have any objection to your drinking if you didn't get drunk?"

"No, she used to drink, too. She still does occasionally."

"Well, if you do try it, you may discover that you really can do it. However, you may discover, too, that no matter how hard you try you still get drunk."

"What do you mean?—You mean some guys can't do it?"

"That's right. Some people lose control over their drinking and need help to stay sober. What you need to wonder about here is whether there is *loss of control*. If you have lost control over your drinking, then you are involved in a condition that can only get progressively worse and for which you need help. This is what we call alcoholism. How much do you know about alcoholism?"

"Not very much. I've read and heard about it a little bit."

"Have you ever wondered if your drinking might have gone into alcoholism?"

"Oh, I guess I've thought about it, but not really very seriously."

"Well, this is what you really need to find out. If you have lost control, you are going to need some help with this. And if you find out that you have, we can talk about that. On the other hand, if you haven't lost control, that would be good for you to find out, too."

"How do you go about finding this out?"

"Well, the easiest way is to set a period of time—like three months. Decide how many drinks you feel would be reasonable drinking for you on any given day. Then see if you can stick to that—never any more on any day for any reason. If you've lost control, you won't be able to make it, but if you haven't lost control, you will have no difficulty."

In such an interview we have become acquainted with his thinking and drinking pattern. Quite obviously, alcoholism is evidenced. He has been enabled to talk about his drinking and perhaps for the first time admit he has been troubled about his drinking. We have stayed close to his ego. The loss of control factor has been inserted into his consciousness. He wants and is going to drink some more and the pastor is not interfering with that except by raising the question of loss of control. This phrase "loss of control" he will never forget and his drinking will never again be quite the same. This is part of the "spoiling process." The truth has been communicated in love. The "stage is set" for the real nature of the drinking problem to prove itself to him. No mention is made of "quitting." He isn't there yet. The pastor is meeting him where he is. There is no moralism.

We are able to "wait and see." We may even tell him what we are doing or if he catches on without our telling him, we are prepared to accept the fact, level with him, and move on from there. This is the "acid test." Many alcoholics can quit for months, sometimes a few years, but they are on a dry drunk. Quitting on his own for a period of time proves nothing. It simply allows the alcoholic a period of delay before facing the reality of his alcoholism, and postpones the day of his eventual recovery. He is fighting powerlessness, and therefore is defeated before he decides to quit. Rarely, if at all, can an alcoholic make the "acid test" of what he sets as a reasonable number of drinks a day, never any more, for three months or even less. If he enters into such a plan, it must be because he wants to do this for himself. Otherwise, it is no good. Time will have to be spent with the wife to help her understand alcoholism and the reason for this procedure. If there is any question in the mind of the person with the drinking problem as to whether or not he has alcoholism, the only way to establish this in a reasonably short period of time is to have him continue drinking within agreed upon limits regarding the daily number of drinks. Incidentally, it is interesting to note how many alcoholics, who don't think they are alcoholics, go along with the idea of finding out whether they can control their drinking. Many have never thought of this possibility and seemingly are quite convinced, at least on the conscious level, that they can drink with control. Besides, this allows for more drinking, and that appeals to the alcoholic, since he isn't ready to think seriously about not drinking.

Some pastors may think it strange, even wrong, for a pastor to consider with a person the possibility of controlled drinking. This, however, is essential. Any decision regarding drinking, not drinking, or getting help to keep from drinking, must come from within the person. Furthermore, if he can be a controlled drinker, he shouldn't quit until this fact is established. Then he is free to make a decision as to whether or not he wants to drink, and help can be offered to resolve the problems which lead to his excessive drinking. If he can't be a controlled drinker, then this problem must be allowed to prove itself to him. It's the only way he can really come to accept it. It may even be wise for the pastor to support him in his hope that he can make the "acid test," but always with expressed reservations.

Without question, one crack that has been made in the shell is the realization that some people can't control their drinking. If and when he accepts this as true for himself, then he must come to realize and accept the fact that neither can he quit on his own. We would hope through the counseling relationship to hasten the process of such realization and acceptance.

This fellow may not return for some time, because he feels the pastor knows his drinking problem too well or because he feels he can handle it by himself. However, there is a real possibility that at the end of the interview he will respond to the idea of coming in on some kind of regular basis while he is making an effort to control his drinking or that he will get in touch with the pastor if and when he has trouble again. He knows this is a person with whom he can talk and who will listen and not moralize—a person who is really interested in *him* and also knows something about the kind of drinking problem he has. If he agrees to continue to come in, trouble can be discussed shortly after it occurs. Such immediacy can be of real value. If he doesn't indicate interest in coming in for a while on a regular basis, it is quite certain that as the problem proves itself to him and he feels the need for further information, clarification, or actual help, he will get in touch with the pastor again.

Another reaction may be, "I know I drink too much at times, but I like to drink."

"You like to drink. How do you mean? You mean you like the taste of whiskey?"

"No, I don't really like the taste. I just like to drink."

"You mean you like the way alcohol makes you feel. What alcohol *does* for you."

"Ya, I guess that's it."

"You don't really like to just have a drink then. You want to drink enough so that you feel it."

"That's right. It relaxes me."

"What do you usually drink—straight whiskey, mixed drinks?"

"Oh, I like them all. But usually after work I like to have a few drinks of bourbon and water."

"When you have a drink, do you usually have a double?"

"Ya, I have a couple of doubles or a double and a single. Sometimes a little more." (Usually quite a bit more. At this point it isn't important to know how much he actually drinks. He will usually be drinking more than he says. Rather the information is supporting his statement that he likes to drink because of the way it makes him feel. He likes what alcohol does for him. So do a lot of people who aren't alcoholics, but the typical pattern of the alcoholic is that whenever he drinks, the primary desire is simply a good degree of anaesthesia.)

"You said that sometimes you drink too much. Are you saying that you feel you shouldn't get drunk?"

"That's right."

"It bothers you, then, when you drink too much."

"Yes, it does."

This interview would naturally not end here, but we will not continue.

Significant now is the fact that in this interview he has talked about his drinking in a way he perhaps never has done before. He has said that he drinks primarily for the anaesthetic effects of alcohol. He has indicated without conscious awareness a loss of control and has admitted that his uncontrolled drinking bothers him.

A third possible reaction is, "I know I drink too much sometimes, but I am naturally a real nervous person and it calms my nerves."

"You feel you drink because you are nervous."

"I know that's the reason."

"According to your wife, you end up getting drunk quite a bit of the time. Do *you* feel that you do?"

"That's true, but she exaggerates it."

"How do you mean?"

"Well, I don't know what she told you, but she usually makes it sound like I am drunk most of the time."

"She felt that you were drinking too much almost every night and spent the weekend drinking."

"That's happened, but it *certainly* isn't like that every week. I didn't have anything to drink last night."

"You said you drink to calm your nerves, to relax, and that sometimes you drink too much. When you drink too much on *some* of these nights, do you plan to drink that much or just enough to take the edge off?"

"That's right. I just want to feel relaxed."

"But then you often end up drinking more than that."

It is significant here that the communication didn't end up centering on his "nervousness" but on his drinking. Later on the possibility that the nervousness could be related to the drinking problem may be discussed.

There is another kind of conversation about drinking that is often possible and can be meaningful. This would be with a person who has scheduled an appointment because of his drinking, or a person who, after some resistance, is now readily talking about his drinking.

"When did *you* first find yourself becoming concerned about your drinking?"

"Oh, about three years ago—maybe five years ago."

"Up until then you weren't particularly concerned about your drinking."

"No. Oh, I have always drunk quite a bit, but I could always handle it," or "No, I have always drunk, but it never was a problem before then."

"Anything happen about then that resulted in your starting to drink more?"

"No, not particularly. Oh, my wife and I weren't getting along too well."

"How do you mean?" (This then would be explored a little bit.)

"What particularly caused you to be concerned about your drinking then?"

"Well, for one thing, I started drinking too much regularly, like every weekend."

"This was new as far as your drinking was concerned?"

"Yes. Oh, I used to drink a lot at special parties, etc., but not every weekend."

"You are getting drunk more often when you don't plan to, is that it?"

"Yes."

"How have you got that figured out?"

"I haven't. And that's what bothers me."

"How much do you know about alcoholism?"

"Not very much."

"Have you ever wondered whether this might be your problem?" (Because more is being written and read on alcoholism, many people with a drinking problem have wondered about it.)

"Well, I've thought about it. But, I don't know."

This would continue with talk about the possibility of loss of control. This he needs to find out. The reason he needs to find out is that if he has "lost control," this is his immediate problem. If he hasn't (chances are he has), then we will center on the apparent marriage problem. In other words, we have heard and recognized the indication of a marriage problem, but if *loss of control* is present, he needs to understand why this is his "immediate problem." Then his drinking is no longer just problem drinking. It is the illness of alcoholism. At this point we would begin to involve the wife both in regard to the alcoholism and the apparent marriage problem.

We come now to a new kind of situation and conversation that could be a quite typical situation for a pastor in a parish setting.

The spouse has been in to see the pastor about her husband's drinking problem. He has listened to her, shared some basic information with her about alcoholism and touched on the main points covered in Chapter VI.

He asked the spouse if her husband knew she had this appointment. With some note of alarm she said that he didn't and if he found out there would be a big explosion. The pastor, however, helped her to understand and accept the fact that she needed to let her husband know. She could simply tell him that she has been so concerned about his drinking and herself that she decided she had to talk to someone. In case the husband then didn't ask her what the pastor said, she was told to say something like this: "You know, after I was through telling the pastor how I felt about the whole situation, he said, "Do you think Joe would come in? I sure would like to know *how he feels* about this."

The chances of Joe's coming in following this kind of response from the pastor may be much better than either the pastor or the spouse might expect.

A first interview with Joe could go like this:

"Hello, Joe, I am glad you decided to come in to see me. How are you feeling?"

Pause

"I guess you know why your wife came in to see me, and I guess you know how she feels about your drinking." (Getting to the point quickly usually is a good idea.)

Pause

"Well, after listening to her, I wanted to find out *how you see it* and *how you feel about your drinking.*"

"Well, I don't know what all she told you, but I am sure it isn't like she says. Listening to her you would think I were drunk most every day."

"She did say she felt you were drinking way too much, but how do you see it, Joe? How would you describe your drinking?"

"Well, I know I drink too much sometimes, but it isn't as bad as she says. In fact, if she wouldn't be on my back all the time, I probably wouldn't be drinking as much as I do."

"How long has this been going on?"

"What, my drinking?"

"No, your wife being on your back about your drinking."

"Oh, about the last two to three years."

"How long have you been drinking?"

"Oh, I've been drinking for years."

"But it is just the last few years that she has really been on your back about your drinking?"

"Yes, I don't know what's gotten into her. Maybe it's menopause. She has gotten more nervous the last few years."

"But she says it's because you're drinking more, is that right?"

"Yes, that's right, but my drinking isn't as bad as she says."

"Joe, you said that you know you drink too much sometimes. How do you mean?"

He now gives a description of what he means, which will very likely include minimizing his actual drinking.

"I gather from what you have said that you don't feel too good about some of the drinking you do. Is that correct?"

"Yes, that's right."

"Why do you think you sometimes drink in ways you don't like?"

"Like I said, she gets on my back and then I just feel, the hell with it."

"Well, Joe, the real question is whether you drink that way sometimes, because of your wife's being on your back, or because you have lost control over your drinking."

"No, that's not it. I can quit anytime. I've proven that."

"I'm not talking about quitting, Joe. I am raising the question as to whether you may be describing loss of control."

"What do you mean? I guess I don't follow you."

"Well, some people lose control over their drinking. They aren't able to just drink in ways that they like to drink. They just aren't able to control their drinking. Instead of quitting, have you ever tried controlling your drinking?"

"How do you mean?"

"It's pretty obvious that you like to drink. It's also pretty obvious that there is a kind of drinking you do that you don't like. Right?"

"That's right."

"Well, have you ever tried to see if you can control your drinking and keep your drinking from getting out of hand? For instance, what do you feel is reasonable drinking for you? On a given day what do you think would be reasonable? Forget about your wife now—just you. How many drinks?"

"I don't know."

"Well, what do you think?"

"Oh, three or four, I suppose, maybe five sometimes."

"When I talk about number of drinks now, I am thinking of a bottle of beer, or a drink—not doubles."

"Yes, that's right."

"O.K. Now do you think you could go for three months never drinking any more than that on any day, for any reason?"

"Yes, I think I could."

"Well, this is the way to find out if you have lost control. Some people lose control over their drinking—about one out of fifteen people who drink. We don't know why, they just do. Then we have a condition that can't get better, it can only get worse. If you, Joe, for instance are drinking too much sometimes because your wife is on your back, that's one thing. But if, without knowing it, you are drinking that way because you have lost control over your drinking, that's something else. Then you have a progressive illness called alcoholism, for which you need help. Then we are talking about this chart. [*See inside back cover.*] So you see, this is the first thing you need to find out. How would you feel about seeing if you could control your drinking for three months?"

"That sounds fine with me." (Even if he didn't respond positively, the idea of control or loss of control will stay with him.)

"Now what did you say you felt would be a reasonable limit— four or five drinks?"

"Yes, about four or five."

"O.K. Now remember, this means never any more than five on any day for any reason—even if your wife is on your back—for three months. If you haven't lost control, you will be able to make that. If you have lost control, you won't be able to make it. It really is that simple.

"Now, how about your wife? Do you want to tell her about this idea, or do you want me to explain it to her? What do you think? Or maybe the three of us should talk about it" Pause.

"O.K. And how would you feel about setting an appointment for a couple of weeks from now or giving me a call just to talk about how it is going?"

Usually the person will follow up and frequently by the end of two weeks he will relate some severe drinking. If he then still has a question about loss of control, another try at control can be a good idea. Within a month, many times the pastor is now with validation able to say, "Joe, there's no question as far as I am concerned that your drinking has gone into alcoholism, and the sooner you are ready to accept this and seek help the better for you. You can be quite sure the progression as shown on that chart will more and more evidence itself in your life if you continue drinking."

At this point a treatment facility or A.A. can be mentioned. If he responds positively the suggestion might be that he try A.A. That may do it. However, if he finds out that he just can't get off the drinking, then he really should consider a treatment facility that will help him get squared away so he can stay sober in A.A.

The alcoholic should be told that many, because of our present knowledge about alcoholism and because of the help available, have accepted their problem and are seeking help much earlier in the progression than has been true in past years. Today A.A. has many members in their thirties and forties, and even some in their twenties; whereas, years ago the members were all older, having gone through the complete progression of alcoholism.

There is the situation in which it is obvious that this is going to be a "one shot deal." The person isn't at all ready to do anything about his drinking or to even seriously talk about it. However, this doesn't always mean that nothing can be accomplished in the first and only appointment.

Here is a young man who has come in under duress and only to satisfy his wife. He has been very successful in his profession, money is no problem, and he is in a position where he can do his work and still have plenty of time for drinking during the day. He says that he likes to drink. He talks about his capacity to earn money. He doesn't know what his wife has to complain about. Anything she wants she can have. If he wants to drink, that's his business.

The facts are that he regularly starts drinking at noon and frequently doesn't get home until after one o'clock in the morning, well loaded, and sometimes in a blackout. His wife does have things, but she doesn't have a husband with whom she can relate.

Some brief exploration was made into his drinking, because he was obviously in a hurry and very hostile. The remark was made, "As I listen to you talk about your drinking, I find myself wondering if you have *lost control.*"

"What do you mean by that?"

An explanation was made.

"Well, I know *I* can control my drinking!"

"If you can, fine, but it's something you need to wonder about because if you can't, you are in more serious trouble than you realize."

"I've always been able to handle any problem I bumped into, and if this is a problem, I'll handle that, too."

"What you actually are going to find out is that if you have lost control, you will discover that this is the first problem you've bumped into that you won't be able to handle by yourself."

"Well, we will see about that."

Significant here again is the fact that "loss of control" has been inserted into his consciousness. His drinking will never be the same again. There is a good chance that without telling anyone he is going to try to see if he can control his drinking. The next day he will have a few, and maybe the next, and then all of a sudden he enters the bar and is still there at one o'clock in the morning. It will be harder now for him to fool himself as completely as he did before.

Incidentally, there is something here that can often be very effective. That is simply wondering out loud, as a person describes his drinking, if he doesn't know he is describing loss of control. "As I listen to you talk about your drinking, I find myself wondering whether there might be loss of control here." That usually opens the door to some further communication in talking about the nature of loss of control and further reflection upon his drinking and how he really feels about it.

If you visit with an alcoholic who is in the hospital because of drinking, there is no sense avoiding this reality even if he doesn't let you know. Somewhere in the conversation you can say, "Bill, how long have you been having a problem with alcohol?" and then proceed to talk about it with him.

Sharing Awareness

It is possible, as we have said, for an alcoholic in a state of compliance to gain and benefit from insights which can be of real value in leading to, as well as following, the surrender phenomenon. We may find it worth while at some time in the counseling process, after a good relationship has been established and alcoholism is obviously evident and has been talked about, to communicate some of our awareness to the alcoholic. Some examples of this kind of communication are as follows.

"You know, Bill, it is very obvious that consciously you don't want to drink. And I get the feeling that you are genuinely puzzled by why you keep drinking and can't really give yourself to what you know you need for your sobriety. What this probably indicates is that although you want sobriety, there is another part of you, which you are unaware of, that is still resisting. A part of you is saying 'yes' and another part of you is saying 'no.' Do you ever have the feeling that you seem to be a divided self?" (Pause)

"This is a painful condition. I know that. It's at times like this that we wish we could press a button and there would be complete acceptance. But it doesn't work like that. It looks as if you probably are just going to have to drink some more."

(Here we are sharing the phenomenon of compliance against surrender in language and in relationship to his feeling experience that he can understand. The news that he will probably have to drink some more usually will be very disturbing but realistically so.)

"How is it going with your drinking? Are you still able to get a good effect—real relief—from drinking? Is it still really working for you? Or are you finding that there is less and less relief and more and more distress in your drinking?"

"Joe, it is very obvious to me that you have lost control over your drinking and you are not going to lick this by yourself. You are going to find that things will get worse, and, really, the sooner you accept the fact that you need outside help to arrest your drinking, the better for you. Your drinking days are over and have been for some time, only you haven't accepted this fact yet. I think that under-neath you know this."

"It is pretty obvious to me that if you could get on top of this thing, you would have done it a long time ago. I am sure you have tried, haven't you?"

"When is the last time you found yourself liking the guy you saw in the mirror?" (Pause) "I know you don't like yourself be-cause of your drinking and you would like to get your self-respect back again. Hopefully, you will soon reach the point where you will feel that your life is worth living, and decide that you don't want to hurt yourself any more. You've had enough of that."

"What do you feel bothers you the most—the fact that you have to give up drinking or the fact that you have bumped into something you can't lick?"

"Have you ever bumped into anything you couldn't lick before?"

"What's your biggest resentment?"

"What do you feel is primary with you now? The feeling that you should do something about your drinking or the feeling that you want to?"

If you are seeing an alcoholic who has had a period of sobriety, started drinking again, and is bitter at everybody and everything, let him ventilate. Then this kind of reflection may be of value. "You know, Jack, I suspect the guy you really hate the most right now is yourself."

"You feel that you have accepted the fact that you are powerless over alcohol. Do you think you have accepted the fact that your life has become unmanageable?"

This kind of communication may bring certain realities he is experiencing into his consciousness and out for discussion. He may be quite surprised to learn that the pastor has this kind of awareness.

There are occasions when the alcoholic doesn't want to talk about his alcoholism, but the "causes" of it. Frequently this can be an expression of the subtle desire to find a way to drink with control. There should be discussion regarding the fact that we really don't know the causes, but we do know what alcoholism is and what is essential for recovery. Whatever the underlying causes, the *immediate* reason for the drinking is *loss of control*. This he needs to understand. After this is adequately discussed, there can be value in talking about some of his basic underlying problems, with the realization that some of these could well be symptoms of alcoholism that are "par for the course" that will diminish in his recovery from alcoholism. It is difficult, in other words, to know sometimes what is what until the drinking problem is taken care of.

With some alcoholics, also, we may become aware that the most helpful move at a certain time is to terminate the counseling relationship after it has gone on for some time. If the alcoholic has good understanding of alcoholism, but is still unable to surrender, it may be that the only way to surrender is through more drinking. He may also be fooling himself and the counselor by telling himself, even while continuing to drink, that he is doing something about his drinking through seeing the pastor and going to A.A. Timing here is an extremely important factor. If and when the pastor does take this step, it is essential that the alcoholic not feel rejected as a person. The conversation might go something like this:

"You know, Joe, it seems to me that for some reason, although you know you are an alcoholic, you can't really accept it yet. You see me regularly, but you aren't going to A.A. You continue to drink, but you aren't ready yet to seek the help you need to stay sober."

Or if he is also going to A.A., the pastor will point up that he is going, but obviously not yet making use of the Twelve Steps and the meetings to stay sober:

"I wonder if you aren't telling yourself that you are doing something about your drinking by seeing me and going to A.A. meetings, and in the process actually fooling yourself. It looks to me as if there isn't much that A.A. or I can do right now for you in regard to your drinking. I think that you are probably going to just have to drink some more until you will be able to quit fighting your alcoholism and really accept it. Maybe, since this is the way it looks, it would be better for you not to see me for a while and possibly even quit going to A.A. meetings until you feel that you really are ready to do something about your drinking."

This frank appraisal of his situation usually gets an alcoholic all "shook up" in a healthy sort of way. Learning that he is going to have to do some more drinking before he is ready to quit, and that the pastor is both aware of this and allowing him freedom to do it, can have positive effects upon him and the counseling relationship.

A word now about women alcoholics. Frequently it is felt that they are "different." They are not. They are people. If they are perceived as being different, the relationship with the woman alcoholic takes on a different nature and becomes a detriment in the helping process. All that we have said applies equally to the women—the phoniness and all other feeling and behavior reactions. It is a source of pain as well as relief when they discover or are confronted with these realities within themselves, but this process and this experience are essential. Perhaps there is one essential difference, and that is the possibility of more intense feelings of shame.

One factor in the processes we have been describing here is that this is not treatment for alcoholism. This is having a relationship and conversation with an alcoholic that hopefully will hasten the day when he will accept treatment. One of the primary goals is to help the alcoholic more quickly to reach the point where he will be ready to accept a referral into treatment whether it be directly to A.A. or to a hospital, clinic, or treatment center, and then into A.A.

Some Practical Considerations

In dealing with alcoholics, the pastor will face certain common situations about which he needs to be aware.

For instance, there is the alcoholic who insists, with great remorse, that his utter sinfulness causes his drinking. Usually with this conviction there exists either the feeling that God cannot forgive him or else the desire to be forgiven and drink no more. There are those who at such a time feel they received God's grace in Jesus Christ and were restored through a "Christian conversion experience." However, with many an alcoholic, such a religious experience at such a time is often more of emotion than of faith and is followed by a return to the bottle. It is not uncommon to find real resistance in such a person when he is confronted with the reality of "loss of control" and the need to accept and responsibly do something specific about his drinking. He will often freely express his guilt, remorse, and sinfulness, but become quite evasive when asked what he intends to *do* about the drinking problem that is making him feel this way. The pastor needs to be aware that the alcoholic can unconsciously use such a reaction to escape facing the hard facts.

When A.A. is first brought up with the alcoholic, he may indicate that he has been to A.A. or known people in A.A., and that it's not for him. It may be that he has been exposed to poor A.A. or poor examples in A.A. Chances are quite good, though, that he just wasn't ready to find out what it really was and what it had to offer him.

He may really have no idea as to what he is saying "no" to. Rather than just drop the subject, it should be talked about in terms of the real nature of A.A., the Twelve Steps, etc., so that he hopefully has some awareness as to what he is saying "no" to.

For instance, the A.A. way of life calls for:

1. Acceptance of reality
2. Faith
3. Commitment of life to the care of God
4. Honesty with God, self, and others
5. Desire and readiness to change one's way of life
6. Asking God for help
7. Making amends
8. Spiritual growth
9. Sharing

That's a lot to say "no" to and it is good for the alcoholic at some point in the counseling to be confronted with the realities he is rejecting. Frequently, this can lead to some significant reflection and discussion.

For some alcoholic it may be that the best thing to do is to directly kick the supports out from under him, gently or not so gently. We don't accept his rationalizations and alibis. We aren't fooled by him, even if he is fooling himself. We will not pamper him or allow an unhealthy dependency to develop. If he gets into serious trouble because of his drinking, we will be concerned with how he feels about his drinking rather than with trying to "fix" anything for him. In a relationship that is kept on this basis, the alcoholic will continually find that he must face the reality of alcoholism and its many problems.

The pastor may wonder what to do when called on by a severely intoxicated alcoholic. Some pastors have spent hours, even into the early morning, talking with a person in such condition. This is of little value. Sometimes it may be necessary for a severely intoxicated alcoholic to be hospitalized to get off the alcohol. This would be helping him more than simply talking endlessly with him in his drunken state. If he is fairly coherent or just coming off a bender, there may be good reason to spend some time with him—at such times the alcoholic is vulnerable and quite accessible. Even so, in many cases, it is best for the pastor to suggest that he call when he is sober. Chances are that when he is sober, the alcoholic won't call, but the pastor could nevertheless call him, remind him of his call while drinking, and what had been said. The pastor may inquire as to whether or not the alcoholic feels the need for help now. Very likely he won't, but this just may be a way to begin exploring his drinking problem with him.

There are times of great anxiety when it is good for the alcoholic to talk and when he actually needs to talk with someone. For this we should try to be available with sacrifice, if necessary. However, he should clearly understand that we will see him at such times *whenever possible*. If it is not possible, then another time can be set or arrangements made for him to talk with someone in A.A. He should have a sponsor. Here, of course, enters the danger that excessive dependency may develop. If, however, these crisis periods are properly handled by the pastor or sponsor, they can be significant strengthening experiences for the alcoholic.

The rule about giving money to alcoholics depends on whom you ask. It is seldom necessary to do this. Usually the alcoholic who has surrendered will not ask for money—which is another way of saying that usually, though not always, the one who does ask is still not ready to do something about his drinking. Money given and not returned may also create a barrier within the alcoholic in relationship to the pastor. And since the immediate need of the alcoholic is seldom money, a good rule is to not give money. Actually the giving of money is usually more a result of the counselor's need than the alcoholic's. At such a time, if he wants to quit drinking but is unable to do so, hospitalization should be considered.

The question is frequently asked, "Should a pastor seek out someone in his parish who he knows is an alcoholic?" The answer usually given is no. But if we believe that alcoholism is a "sickness unto death," the worst thing we can do is to do nothing. The pastor can try to schedule an appointment in his office with this person by simply saying, "I would like to see you. Could we set up an appointment?" If the alcoholic doesn't come in, the pastor can try to go to him.

When he sees the alcoholic, after some general conversation he may begin by saying, "I've heard that you may have (or that you are having) a problem with drinking, and I would like to talk with you about it. Do you feel you have a problem with your drinking, or how do you feel about it?" Then some of the methods previously mentioned can be used to get him to reflect about his drinking and to raise the question of the possibility and nature of loss of control. If he is completely resistant, the pastor can say, "If you ever begin to think that your drinking is a problem, feel free to call me, because help is available." In the process, the alcoholic has sensed some concern and understanding, has gained some knowledge about alcoholism even if the word wasn't used, and has had his drinking significantly spoiled so that it will never be exactly the same again— which is to say that, properly handled, even if he is resistant, the alcoholic has been helped.

We now turn to the question that becomes the vital question in the counseling process: What can be some of the signs that the surrender phenomenon has taken place? In this connection, we strongly urge the reading of the reprints of talks by Dr. Tiebout listed in the recommended readings.

A pastor learns to sense, although all too often inaccurately, when an alcoholic has quit fighting, given in, and, consciously and unconsciously, accepted his powerlessness. His rationalization, defiance, and projection quite suddenly and miraculously disappear. I say miraculously, because these have been behavior patterns of long standing. When they disappear, the change from the old pattern is so obvious that the alcoholic seems to be "a different person." It is true, though, that an alcoholic in a state of submission may give the appearance of surrender. Experience in working with alcoholics in both states makes it possible in many cases to discern whether there might be real surrender or just submission.

Experience teaches that with surrender plans disappear—plans about all he needs to do, plans to "fix it" with his wife, plans to go out and make money and thus restore his self-esteem (a common thought in the unsurrendered alcoholic after a binge). Rather he is concerned primarily or only with doing something about his drinking. He knows for the first time that if he can take care of this problem, he will be able to face other problems with the attitude expressed in the prayer, "God grant me the serenity to accept things I cannot change, the courage to change things I can, and the wisdom to know the difference."

A very basic indication is the living of the 24-hour program suggested by A.A. This involves the prayer for help from God in the morning which is recognition of his own powerlessness that day and a prayer of gratitude at the end of the day. When this begins to become mechanical or sincerity in prayer ceases, surrender is on the way out or has already disappeared. Together with this way of life and such prayers, many alcoholics in a state of surrender will have a period of private meditation each day. And, of course, inherent in this is regular attendance at a weekly A.A. meeting, more if necessary, not only because he *has* to, but because he *wants* to.

In the state of surrender the alcoholic is honest with himself about himself and his drinking. This is noticeably different from the dishonesty, rationalization, and projection typical of the "alcoholic thinking." If he makes a typical rationalizing or projecting statement, he will now catch and correct himself. He might, for example, make a comment like this:

"You know, I started drinking when I was in the service. Booze was always available, everybody drank, so naturally I . . . no, that 'so naturally' shouldn't be there. Nobody forced me to drink." He will be looking at his drinking problem in terms of himself and will see that essentially his thinking and his feelings caused the difficulty and not something or someone outside himself. In other words, he will be humble as well as honest. If the old "alcoholic thinking" appears and he is in danger of drinking, he will, if he is in a state of surrender, begin to think consciously the thoughts he needs to think and do the things he needs to do in order to keep from drinking. Those who have worked with alcoholics know what a stupendous switch all this is, but nobody knows it better than the surrendered alcoholic.

Another evidence of surrender can be the desire to take Steps 4 and 5—to make a thorough, searching, honest moral inventory and to admit the defects found, to God, to self, and to another person. The alcoholic who is in a state of submission and not surrender usually resists this. He will usually just avoid these steps. If some pressure is put on him, he will always be in the process of "getting at it" or else, in "doing it," he will end up with a very poor inventory which is easily recognizable where one has seen honest accomplishment of these steps. It is important to realize, however, that the inability to do a good 4th and 5th Step can also be an indication of deep-seated emotional problems.

In one specific case, there was some question as to whether or not a particular alcoholic was in a state of real surrender or just submission. He showed some positive changes. His inventory and 5th Step even sounded quite good except when it came to the section on dishonesty. Here he gave a very insignificant example that was quite unrelated to the basic dishonesty in his alcoholic thinking. Furthermore, his primary concern was that he be reconciled with his wife. If this happened, then he could make it. Reconciliation with his wife was for him the primary immediate problem rather than his powerlessness over alcohol. These two factors in his thinking indicated no real surrender. When things didn't work out the way he thought they needed to and should, particularly when his wife wouldn't take him back, he got drunk.

However, after that drunk the surrender phenomenon began to evidence itself. He found himself a more permanent place to stay which evidently, as one looks back, meant that he was accepting the reality of being separated from his wife. This he describes as "one of the most difficult things I have ever done in my life."

When she brought him some things he needed, he was angry, depressed, complaining, and took them without saying thanks. At that point it looked as if there was not surrender. But because there actually was surrender, he realized that he hadn't even thanked his wife for her kindness and became conscious of what a jerk he was. He immediately sought to get in touch with her to tell her he was sorry, and continued in his efforts to reach her until he succeeded. She said later, "That's the first apology I have had from him in ten years," and he was able to say that he felt better for having told her he was sorry.

He recognized this reaction on his part as something new. In describing what usually would have been his reaction, he said that he would have thought of the fact that he hadn't said thanks and that this was wrong, but immediately he would have proceeded to tell himself that she had been wrong many times too. In fact, he would have thought, if it weren't for her being wrong, he wouldn't be in the place he was. Then he would have started drinking.

When a person is in a state of surrender, the honest thoughts he needs to think when he is headed for trouble come into his consciousness and are accepted and acted upon. This is illustrated in the case of the alcoholic discussed above. During the time that this man was unable to reach his wife, he was depressed. In a state that he knew inevitably led to drinking, he went to the A.A. club and talked with another alcoholic while also calling a counselor to whom he had been referred. That which followed was a more honest evaluation of himself, including such things as awareness that he could do less on his own than he thought, and that he needed more help than he thought; awareness that he had never had any feeling for another person and realization that he had to begin thinking of others; and awareness that he had not given of himself or assumed necessary responsibilities in his relationship with other people. Whereas he had never before enjoyed going to the A.A. club, he now said that "they are beginning to look like people." Anyone who has worked much with alcoholics and seen how completely bound up within themselves and their own little world they can be, will know the significance of that last statement. It indicated that some-thing totally new was taking on reality within him as a result of the surrender phenomenon.

Unfortunately, it is possible for the alcoholic who has surrendered to cease being a surrendered person and have a slip at sometime. However, slips don't "just happen" even though many an alcoholic likes to think they do. As Dr. Tiebout says, the omnipotent Ego has asserted itself again, and with this, dishonesty and pride go to work. After the slip has occurred, the pastor must give the alcoholic an opportunity to express and explore his feelings. He must at the same time inform the alcoholic of some very basic practical factors that are part of the process leading to a slip. Without exception, the alcoholic skips or doesn't pray sincerely the morning prayer of sur-render on the day he drinks. Usually he has been skipping it for days before he drank. Rather than ask if he quit his morning prayer, the pastor may simply ask, "How long before you started drinking did you quit praying your morning prayer?" He may say, "I know what you mean." If he did pray, he was not sincere. The daily inventory, attendance at A.A. and church, the way he handled resentments, and the involvement with his family that followed surrender had very likely disappeared or deteriorated before he started drinking. However, the alcoholic who slips has either never been made aware of these "danger signals" or else has unconsciously blocked them out and would react with strong feeling if someone else pointed them out to him. If he had had these in his conscious awareness, he would have done something positive to keep from drinking. Unconsciously, however, he wanted to drink, so unconsciously he blocked out the obvious danger signals and in time proceeded to get drunk.

There is an interesting little incident that points up this blocking process very clearly. An alcoholic in A.A. had established for him-self the plan of walking to work each day by a certain route which took him by a church. If he had forgotten his morning prayer of surrender and the acceptance of his powerlessness, he would be reminded as he saw the church. For some time prior to taking a drink, he walked a different route to work without realizing what he was doing. When he later sought to figure out why he had slipped, he became aware of the fact that this was just the final of many danger signals that were unconsciously blocked out of his consciousness.

Perhaps one of the most basic factors contributing to this process is the need for the alcoholic to become dishonest with himself before he can take a drink. After he has had a slip, he must search out evidence of this dishonest thinking. Usually, when he does this, he will discover that he began to be dishonest with himself long before he drank. Any slip, of course, requires another 4th or 5th Step.

After the slip, it is also important for the pastor to help the alcoholic see other important factors that caused him to take that first drink. Certain "danger signals" such as those mentioned above are warnings to all alcoholics, but many alcoholics discover certain others that are peculiarly their own. When the alcoholic notices such signs, he should see them as clear indication that he needs to take stock of himself and talk with the pastor, his sponsor, or some other understanding person. If danger signals are evident to the pastor but unnoticed by the alcoholic, the pastor should perhaps talk this over with the alcoholic. Nothing can be lost in so doing—if he is going to get drunk, he will anyway, and there is always the possibility that the drunk can be avoided. Sometimes the approach may be a direct statement of the facts. Sometimes a question such as, "Are you aware of . . . . ?" or "Have you wondered if you might be headed for trouble?"

A few concrete examples here may be helpful in showing how slips are avoided when the alcoholic is in the state of surrender. One alcoholic forgot, when he awoke in the morning, to go through the conscious act of accepting his powerlessness and humbly asking God for strength for the day. That forenoon at work his boss gave him a sack lunch and sent him off by himself to work on a house.

At noon when he opened the sack, together with the sandwiches there were two bottles of beer. By this time he wasn't only hungry; he was also thirsty. His immediate conscious thought was: "Nobody will know." But because he was in the state of surrender he also thought, "I may get by with it this time and maybe even the next time, but eventually it will get me." For some minutes the thoughts that would lead him to drinking struggled against the thoughts that would keep him from drinking. Without surrender present there would have been no struggle—the thoughts that would help him not to drink would have been unconsciously blocked out. But because this man had surrendered unconsciously as well as consciously and didn't want to drink, he became aware of having forgotten his morning meditation and prayer. He spent a few moments in meditation and never drank the beer.

Another illustration is found in the experience of the man who slipped after forgetting his morning prayer for help. At a later date he again realized that he was forgetting his morning meditation and prayer. He had gotten a good-paying job as truck driver. Surrender resulted in his realizing what had happened. He handled the problem by attaching a copy of his prayer in the cab of the truck where he would see it each morning, in case he needed a visual reminder. Such a procedure is not to be scoffed at in the early days and months of sobriety for some alcoholics.

With the alcoholic who is making significant progress, praise may not be completely withheld, but it should not be given freely and generously. Many alcoholics have an excessive need for approval and praise. As proof of this, there are the classic stories about alcoholics who got drunk just as they were about to attain a long-sought goal such as a major promotion.

Finally there must be realistic goals and necessary limits. In the description of the "one shot deal," the goal was quite realistic and also very limited. With an ongoing relationship, goals must be perceived in terms of a process that involves, in many cases, months and even years. We are hoping because of the relationship that the period of time leading to the surrender phenomenon will be shortened.

This leads to the importance of setting limits. Limits are not only obviously necessary for the pastor in terms of time available, but also essential for the alcoholic. Working with a few alcoholics doesn't have to be a very time-consuming experience. Hour appointments can be set on a weekly or biweekly basis. There are very few real "emergency" situations. The pastor and the alcoholic who is being seen regularly can readily perceive situations as being "emergencies" when in reality they are not. A call may come from an alcoholic:

"Can I see you today?"

"What's the trouble?"

"Well, I've bumped into a real problem at work . . ." (This is briefly discussed).

"Let's see, Joe. You have an appointment with me Thursday (or next week). Why don't we wait until then and we can talk about it. Okay?"

If a pastor is spending excessive time with alcoholics, this is usually an indication of a problem within the pastor. This is just "a part of" his ministry. Chances are he is also spending excessive time with other people and other parts of his ministry, but little or no time with his wife and family. So there are two people who need help, the pastor and the alcoholic.

Limits also need to be set in terms of the alcoholic having to be responsible for his problem and not being allowed to be over-dependent upon the pastor.

In connection with goals and limits, there may be the severely deprived, very emotionally sick alcoholic who needs at least one person with whom he can have a relationship on an ongoing basis with specific limits set, like an hour a week or an hour every two weeks. There is little hope of anything happening in the relationship other than concern and support. At least he has someone with whom he can relate. Someone who cares. Psychiatrically, even if he has the money, the prognosis is poor. And yet maybe some day a miracle will happen because of a meaningful relationship.

There is one such case in which there was a severe and deep emotional deprivation throughout life. Periods of this person's life were spent on skid rows in major cities of the country. There were some comparatively brief periods of sobriety holding down a job. This person had no close friend. He was seen by the pastor for an hour once a week or every other week. After awhile the pastor said that he would not talk to him on the phone when he was drunk. However, if he came in for his appointment drunk, he was seen for an hour.

It looked as if it would just go on this way as long as the man was around. Then one day he went to a treatment center consisting of alcoholism counselors where he had been before. Something happened and he was sober until he died. When asked what had happened, he said he wasn't sure, but he thought one of the significant things was that one of the counselors said one day, "You know, Pete (not his real name), you have forgotten to be grateful in your life." This never entered the pastor's mind, and if it had, he probably never would have said it, knowing this man's deprived history.

He found a group in A.A. that warmly received him and fully accepted him. Frequently, he talked about how wonderful it was to have such friends and with particular meaning while he was in the hospital dying.

Dealing with Tension Periods

It seems that many alcoholics have regular periods of days, sometimes weeks, when tension, anxiety, and depression are extremely high. They may not have learned that other people do too (though, granted perhaps, with lesser intensity) and that if they ride them through, the severe tension will subside *even if they don't get drunk*. Most alcoholics who are just setting out on the road to recovery haven't learned this because at all such previous times they have gotten drunk. Even though they suffered much pain, remorse, guilt, and self-hatred in the hangover, the binge took care of the initial basic pain. The longer the period of sobriety and the more of these tension-periods "toughed out," the less frequent, severe, and lasting they usually become. This is good for the alcoholic to know.

These periods may be extreme depression for some and cause such a sense of isolation that the alcoholic finds it impossible to be involved in or benefit from any kind of personal relationship. He loses all interest in people that he normally likes and in things he needs to do. An alcoholic doesn't often talk about how he really feels at such a time. If it seems that this is what he went through before his last drunk, it is well to share with him the awareness that there are other alcoholics who also go into such a "deep dip." He may be helped by knowing this and by knowing that someone else is concerned and senses how rough it must be. Attempts at referral to a psychiatrist should be made when such depression is in evidence.

It can be of real value, too, for the alcoholic to not only tell himself that the milder depression will go away *even if he doesn't drink,* but to understand that during such periods he needs to avoid tension-producing situations as much as possible. When confronted with this problem, the pastor needs to decide if this is for him or some other professional person to handle.

Additional Counseling

What we have been saying about counseling has essentially and with purpose been in regard to the alcoholic who has no deeply severe underlying emotional disorder. We have purposely concentrated on those whose primary problem is alcoholism because they are the ones whom pastors can most readily help in conjunction with the spiritual insights and recovery steps of A.A. But, again, it is important not to categorize all alcoholics as *just* alcoholics. Awareness and sensitivity are of vital importance in detecting the presence of another severe disorder.

Once an alcoholic has surrendered, he will be able to benefit from further counseling in regard to other problems, individual and marital. He will be open to becoming aware of his egocentricity, hostility, over-dependency, and failure to assume responsibility for his feelings. He will be open to the awareness that when he began to turn to alcohol, he ceased to grow emotionally and spiritually as a responsible person. This then becomes a typical pastoral counseling situation which may or may not necessitate psychiatric care, depending upon the pastor and the severity of the problems. Often group therapy is most beneficial. With some, however, it is best to let them concentrate just on sobriety for a reasonable period of time.

An unmet need in many areas of the country is an adequate long-term treatment center, both public and voluntary, in which the severely disturbed alcoholic separated from alcohol can receive psychotherapy which hopefully will eventually enable him to benefit from the help that A.A. has to offer. Some of these people, the big A.A. book states, are able to attain sobriety through A.A. alone without such psychiatric treatment. Experiences validate this statement. But many in A.A. who see only the alcoholism do no good by saying to such people, "The only trouble with you is that you are not working the program. You are not being honest." There are alcoholics who have deep emotional disorders together with their alcoholism and who are not going to make it with just A.A. and the help of the pastor.

Certainly, the pastor *should not seek to function alone* in his concern for and counseling with the alcoholic. Besides knowing some A.A. people, he should become acquainted with other resources that exist in his community and state, such as alcoholism information and referral centers, alcoholism clinics and state treatment programs. The county welfare people and the public health nurse may be of assistance. Sometimes psychiatric help is necessary prior to and after the alcoholic's recovery. Physicians and the local hospital are vital resources. If the hospital does not offer treatment for alcoholics, maybe the pastor can help to make this a reality. Finally, we need to recognize and accept that some alcoholics are never going to recover. As we know, this is more difficult than accepting the reality of a terminal illness, such as cancer.

Alcoholics should generally be left with the initiative when referrals are made to A.A., a medical doctor, or a clinic. Give him the name and telephone number and let him call. (When somebody else calls to schedule an appointment for an alcoholic to see you, try to see if you can "fix it" so the alcoholic has to call you.) Sometimes, however, there is value in having the pastor take an alcoholic to meet an A.A. person, to attend his first A.A. meeting, or to introduce him to the doctor or the clinic.

The Alcoholic, the Pastor, and the Church

If the recovering alcoholic who is in A.A. has left the church, it is extremely important that the pastor doesn't anxiously set out to "get" the alcoholic to come to church or to join the church. If there is a meaningful relationship, in time the alcoholic will perhaps begin to raise some questions in this area or the pastor may come to see that the alcoholic has reached the point where his thinking, feeling, and concerns about his relationship with Christ and his church can and should be discussed. There are times when the problem is procrastination, and a direct talk with the alcoholic about his relationship to Christ and the church may be the best approach. But the important factor is for the pastor not to be out in front of the alcoholic in this area so that his own needs rather than the alcoholic's are being met. The pastor's concern for this person must not change into an effort to manipulate him. Given a period of time, many alcoholics will come to a meaningful Christian faith and to meaningful existence within the Christian fellowship.

To be remembered is prayer for the alcoholic and his family both before and during recovery.

Finally, a word should be said about the recovered alcoholic and the wine in Holy Communion. This is the one and only time, place, and experience in which he can take even a small amount of beverage alcohol. If Holy Communion happens to be followed by a drunk, the cause is not the communion wine—the drunk would have occurred anyway. It may take a while before the person feels ready to partake of wine in Holy Communion. Some pastors suggest that he wait until he is ready. Others use grape juice. The context and meaning of Holy Communion is completely different from his use of alcohol as an alcoholic. The pastor should try to help him see this and work through his feelings concerning it. A number of alcoholics find that it is a deeply meaningful experience to partake of that which previously was literally destroying their lives, and which can now be an element in this most significant relationship with their Lord and fellow Christians.

V.

FOURTH AND FIFTH STEPS

One of the most important aspects of the alcoholic's recovery is his accomplishment of the 4th and 5th Steps in the Twelve Steps of A.A. We have already seen that two problems that contribute in a major way to the alcoholic's drinking are dishonest thinking and guilt. For this reason he needs to go through a process and experience that will enable him to look at himself honestly and then admit the truth of his inventory to himself, to God, and to another human being.

The "big A.A. book" has this to say about the 4th and 5th Steps:

"We believe the acts of drunkenness, dishonesty, envy, self-pity, spite, hatred, resentment, malice, and injustice not only injure us, but are the acts of depraved people in the eyes of society and opposed to all spiritual virtues known to A.A. members who have been spiritually awakened. If these be spiritual debits, then most of us have drunk ourselves into spiritual bankruptcy.

"Notwithstanding the great necessity for discussing ourselves with someone, it may be one is so situated that there is no suitable person available. If that is so, this step may be postponed only, however, if we hold in complete readiness to go through with it at the first opportunity. We say this because we are very anxious that we talk to the right person. It is important that he be able to keep a confidence; that he fully understand and approve what we are driving at; that he will not try to change our plan. But we must not use this as a mere excuse to postpone. When we have decided who is to hear our story, we waste no time. We pocket our pride and go to it, illuminating every twist of character, every dark cranny of the past . . . . Once we have taken this Step we are delighted. We can look the world in the eye. We begin to feel the nearness of our Creator. We have had certain spiritual beliefs, but now we begin to have a spiritual experience."[1]

Alcoholics are encouraged to take time with Step 5, but when the time comes, to act promptly. Postponing this step is inconsistent with their plan of recovery. The suggestion is that it is far better to take it before they think they are ready than to postpone it and not take it at all.

Since the trend among many A.A. people seems to be towards taking the 5th Step with an understanding pastor, this is an opportunity for the pastor to render a most significant service. In some areas A.A. people have held seminars to acquaint pastors with the meaning of these Steps and what is involved in an alcoholic's taking his 5th Step. The pastor, hopefully, will look upon the 5th Step as a real pastoral "soul care" relationship for which he must and can find time on his busy schedule whether or not the alcoholic is a member of his congregation. Naturally, as he has more experience with 5th Steps, he will become more skilled in determining what is a good inventory.

It is necessary to first have a session to help an alcoholic understand what the inventory is and how to take his inventory. "Guide to Fourth Step Inventory"[2] is available for the pastor to explain and give to the alcoholic. Section A in this guide is the most essential part of the inventory process and should be discussed thoroughly before proceeding. Emphasis should be placed on an effort to be as honest as possible and on the value of writing out the inventory. A written inventory assures completeness in both the inventory and Fifth Step.

The inventory procedure needs to be talked about in a positive way,

---

[1] *Alcoholics Anonymous*, pp. 74-75
[2] *Guide to Fourth Step Inventory*, Hazelden Foundation, 1961, Center City, Minn.

pointing up the value of taking such an inventory. Hopefully he will benefit by being able to: (1) Get to know himself better; (2) Become more keenly aware of how he needs to change; (3) Recognize danger signals to his sobriety before he takes the first drink; (4) Live more comfortably with himself and others; (5) Have the door opened for a more personal and meaningful relationship with God.

The assumption is that all the defects listed in the guide are present. Therefore the alcoholic must focus on discovering how these defects have been expressing themselves in his life. The list includes: selfishness, alibis, dishonest thinking, pride, resentment, intolerance, envy, phoniness, procrastination, self-pity, feelings easily hurt, and fear. One more should be added to the list—perfectionism. He demands perfection of himself and is also disillusioned when he doesn't find it in others. Since he and others are imperfect humans and can never be perfect, he can never win. He demands of himself and others what God in his Word and life itself reveal is impossible.

His drinking history and overt behavior usually will be included. However, the important thing is to determine the nature of his defects and realize *"this is me."* There should be a listing of at least two or three specific examples of each one. He should also seek to determine his assets, but these he may be able to see more clearly as he continues on the road to recovery.

When the alcoholic is ready for the Fifth Step, sufficient time must be arranged. At least one hour should be set aside, and the pastor should explain from the start that in case more time is needed, another appointment will, of course, be made. If the alcoholic senses that the pastor is in a hurry, he will interpret this as rejection, and a vital experience in his recovery is doomed to failure.

The alcoholic very likely has never gone through this kind of experience before and may be quite anxious. If the pastor feels comfortable and at ease, the alcoholic will feel better. Before the alcoholic actually begins, the pastor should explain that he may be taking some notes on things they will talk about when the alcoholic is finished. As he listens, and the emphasis is on listening, the pastor should remember that some apparent "little thing" may be "big" to the alcoholic. Then, too, he must be "shock-proof." At first he may react to certain comments with a facial expression of surprise or shock which may prevent the alcoholic from really opening up. With experience, this ceases to be a problem.

There will be a great deal of variation in the execution of the Fifth Step. Some individuals will, of course, be more capable than others, but ability is not what counts. The important factor is whether or not there has been an *honest effort* to take a searching and fearless moral inventory. The lack of such an inventory may mean that the alcoholic isn't ready to be or capable of being honest within himself. He may not yet have accepted his powerlessness over alcohol, and until this happens the door to self-honesty remains closed. He may be one of the unfortunate ones who is just incapable of being honest with himself. A.A. refers to such people as those they cannot help. However, many who come with an inadequate Fifth Step are quite capable of being honest with themselves, but aren't yet ready to be.

If the alcoholic is having difficulty in his Fifth Step, the pastor should make an effort to draw him out more. Certain things that are common to alcoholics can be mentioned, for instance, "How about resentments or self-pity? Did these cause you any trouble?" Such leading may help to open him up. If he evades or denies, the pastor can be quite sure that the alcoholic isn't ready for what he is trying to do and should consider this possibility with him.

When he has finished relating his inventory, it is essential to talk about it together. There may be such things as resentments that he hasn't worked through, guilt or other feelings unresolved, certain acts or behavior that he has questions about, his perfectionism. The nature of certain defects he has mentioned may need to be clarified. He needs to make amends to the people he has harmed. Even if the other person involved has forgotten it, the alcoholic hasn't, and for his own sake he needs to make direct amends, if possible, except when to do so would hurt rather than help the other person. Amends to the wife are certainly a must. And above all he needs to make amends to himself in the process of forgiving himself. There may be the matter of money stolen that is known or unknown to persons from whom it was taken. Restitution, if at all possible, is necessary.

Throughout the Fifth Step the alcoholic must be allowed to feel what pain there is for him in this experience. The pastor should neither minimize the gravity of anything he relates nor try to comfort him with reassurance. He wouldn't be seeing the pastor if he weren't willing to face the truth about himself.

For an alcoholic raised in the church, it can be beneficial to reflect with him on the question, "With all of this that you have looked at in yourself, how do you now think God feels towards you?" In discussing this, the pastor has the opportunity to learn where the alcoholic is in his understanding of God and to talk with him about the true nature of God. That his alcoholism and the changes it wrought in him have not been able to change God's attitude toward him, as evidenced, for instance, in the parable of the Prodigal Son, can be a revelation to him. Reference can be made to scriptural truths he learned in childhood, and on this foundation he can begin to build a better understanding of the nature of God's love and grace. With such a person, a pastor may sense that a closing prayer may be meaningful to the alcoholic, and therefore appropriate.

Other alcoholics may still be quite agnostic, and such a reflection with them would certainly not be meeting the person where he is. Some conversation about the simple matter of asking for help each morning and expressing thanks each evening may be helpful.

When we think of this experience as involving the three basic relationships for which man was created—relationship with God, self, and others—the question of confession following the Fifth Step should be considered, particularly with the alcoholic who has been raised in the church. In admitting the truth of his inventory to himself, he is doing that which is necessary in his relationship with himself. In admitting this to another human being he is, in reality, being restored to relationship with his fellow human beings. Private confession and absolution may *for some* be the most significant evidence of restoration in their relationship with God. The pastor may feel that the alcoholic might desire this, but he should exercise caution and not push the alcoholic. A sense of need within the alcoholic must be the determining factor. If the alcoholic decides he would like such a service, it might be best either to have it immediately or to set aside another specific time. It is also suggested that for some the confession and absolution be done before the altar with the pastor in full vestments. Generally, Roman Catholic priests make it clear that the Fifth Step is not confession, and that confession should follow.

When the Fifth Step session is completed, the door should be left open for the alcoholic to come in for further counseling if he feels the need. The possibility of his wanting to take another Fifth Step at a later date can also be mentioned.

There should be some conversation on the importance of Steps 6 and 7 in A.A. following the completion of the Fifth Step.

As has been indicated, many alcoholics in A.A. have not taken Steps 4 and 5. Some think they have done this in their squad meetings. The "big A.A. book" makes it clear that this is not possible. The Fifth Step is made only through a specific appointment with another person after the personal inventory has been taken. It is easy for alcoholics to tell themselves that this isn't important, even though A.A. says this is the beginning of the spiritual experience.

When asked to speak at A.A. meetings, the experienced pastor can place the Fourth and Fifth Steps at the top of his list of possible subjects. If he uses the material in the "big A.A. book" as the basis for his talk, he makes it more difficult for A.A. members to be defensive. The person who is still asking, "Why is this necessary?" or "Is this necessary?" will never know the answer until he takes the steps. The alcoholic who has honestly gone through these steps never asks this question. He knows the answer. All Twelve Steps are written in the past tense, which is an indication that the answer lies in the doing. An alcoholic needs to know that there are some who had trouble and later realized that this trouble was due to not having taken these steps. He also needs to know that there are others who, after some years of sobriety, finally took these steps and realized what they had been missing.

The alcoholic needs more than sobriety. Without the Fourth and Fifth Steps he may have sobriety, but he will have no basic understanding of God's grace and of the spirituality of the A.A. fellowship and recovery. These steps are essential to his emotional and spiritual growth.

VI.

COUNSELING THE SPOUSE

In many cases, the spouse is the key person in the eventual recovery of the alcoholic. As has already been pointed out, counseling prior to the acceptance of his alcoholism can bring the alcoholic to greater awareness, better understanding, and earlier acceptance of his problem. However, even if the alcoholic is not willing to come in on a regular basis, his wife often is; and any guidance that enables her to relate more realistically and positively with her alcoholic husband can have the same effect.

She needs help for herself as well as help in understanding alcoholism. This becomes apparent when we realize what having an alcoholic husband may mean as far as she and the family are concerned. Alcoholism has brought her to a real Gethsemane where the worst is always yet to come.

The anguish and wreckage may include some or all of the following: the destruction of any meaningful kind of relationship and communication; the terrible anxiety of the threat of economic insecurity; eventual loss of job, business, professional practice, or farm; the need for relief or necessity of leaving the children for full-time employment; isolation from friends and social groups; the necessity of assuming the responsibility of both father and mother; lonesome and anxious days and nights with him at home drinking; the destructive feelings of guilt, shame, resentment, sense of failure, and self-pity; taking out her feelings not only on her husband but also on her children; worrying about not only what he is doing to the children, but also what she is doing to them; the bewildering, painful, guilt-producing experiences of having her husband blame her for his drinking and behavior and of being accused of infidelity while he has been gone from home on a drinking spree; feelings of hatred and loss of respect for her husband and yet awareness of the kind of person he could be; the possibility of enduring all this, her husband not recovering, and then facing divorce.

Joan Jackson describes the kind of adjustment some wives go through as the crisis of alcoholism appears and develops. We will give here a brief description of the phases of adjustment, but because what she describes are very common phenomena, we strongly recommend the reading of the entire article for a more thorough description of each phase.

"At the time marriage was considered, the drinking of most of the men was within socially acceptable limits. In a few cases the men were already alcoholics but managed to hide this from their fiancees. They drank only moderately or not at all when on dates, and often avoided friends and relatives who might expose their excessive drinking. The relatives and friends who were introduced to the fiancee were those who had hopes that 'marriage would straighten him out,' and thus said nothing about the drinking. In a small number of cases the men spoke with their fiancees of their alcoholism. The woman had no conception of what alcoholism meant, other than that it involved more than the usual frequency of drinking, and they entered the marriage with little more preparation than if they had known nothing about it.

"Stage 1: Incidents of excessive drinking begin, and although they are sporadic, place strains on the husband-wife interaction. In attempts to minimize drinking, problems in marital adjustment not related to the drinking are avoided.

"Stage 2: Social isolation of the family begins as incidents of excessive drinking multiply. The increasing isolation magnifies the importance of family interactions and events. Behavior and thought become drinking centered. Husband-wife relationship deteriorates and tension rises. The wife begins to feel self-pity and to lose her self-confidence as her behavior fails to stabilize her husband's drinking.

There is an attempt still to maintain the original family structure, which is disrupted anew with each episode of drinking, and as a result the children begin to show emotional disturbance.

"Stage 3: The family gives up attempts to control the drinking, and begins to behave in a manner geared to relieve tension rather than achieve long-term ends. The disturbance of the children becomes more marked. There is no longer any attempt to support the alcoholic in his role as husband and father. The wife begins to worry about her own sanity, and about her inability to make decisions or act to change the situation.

"Stage 4: The wife takes control of the family and the husband is seen as a recalcitrant child. Pity and strong protective feelings largely replace the earlier resentment and hostility. The family becomes more stable and organized in a manner to minimize the disruptive behavior of the husband. The self-confidence of the wife begins to be rebuilt.

"Stage 5: The wife separates from her husband if she can resolve the problems and conflicts surrounding this action.

"Stage 6: The wife and children reorganize as a family without the husband.

"Stage 7: The husband achieves sobriety, and the family which had become organized around an alcoholic husband, reorganizes to include a sober father and experiences problems in reinstating him in his former role."[1]

Many wives, without understanding alcoholism, seek through various ways to get the alcoholic to do something about his drinking. These ways are so common that they have become known as the "home treatment." In the course of counseling, the wife should be shown the futility of such treatment as well as other attitudes and behavior that will hinder instead of help. The following are examples of the home treatment and the reasons for their failure:

---

[1] Joan Jackson, M.A., "The Adjustment of the Family to the Crisis of Alcoholism," reprint from *Quarterly Journal of Alcohol Studies*, Vol. 15, No. 4, December, 1954, pp. 562-586.

1. "Don't you love me? If you really loved me and the children you would do something about your drinking. Don't you realize what you are doing to me and the children and yourself?" To him, this only communicates lack of understanding of how he feels. Nobody is more painfully aware of what he is doing than the alcoholic. His guilt and self-hatred, sense of loneliness, and sense of rejection are intensified.

2. "Why don't you be a man? Use your willpower." Imagine what that does to someone who is already overwhelmed with feelings of inadequacy and who has tried, perhaps unbeknown to others, to do just that and failed. This also further perpetuates that which has to be destroyed—the feeling that if he is really a man, he should be able to use his willpower and quit. He needs instead to come to understand that alcoholism is a sickness, that this is not a matter of willpower but powerlessness, and that there isn't anything shameful or unmanly about accepting this reality and seeking the help he needs for sobriety.

3. Coax him not to drink and exact promises. He will make, but cannot keep, promises. His failure then aggravates his guilt, anxiety, and self-hatred. He is supported in his delusion that he can do it on his own, if he *really* tries.

4. Hide or destroy his supply of alcohol. This is a waste of time and money as the wife soon learns. The same applies to withholding money and telling his friends not to serve him liquor. It is impossible to keep an alcoholic from getting and drinking alcohol.

5. Threats. In most cases the wife will threaten the alcoholic many times, but never be ready to follow through. He begins to sense that she doesn't really mean it. There is a time when threats are both necessary and useful. However, they are not to be used until every other resource has been exhausted.

Usually other factors that are not helpful come into the picture. A "holier than thou" or "martyr-like" attitude isn't healthy for her or for the alcoholic. Sometimes a wife will begin to drink with her husband, thinking that he will then exercise more control. Eventually, this disillusions her and only supports him in his drinking.

If all of this is to be avoided, what is she to do and how can counseling help her? First, it is important that she talk about her problems with someone other than her husband, children, and family. It is important, too, that she sense that this other person knows what she is going through, how difficult and painful it is, and is interested in how she feels. Counseling will give her the opportunity to ventilate and work through her own feelings, while coming to a necessary understanding and acceptance of alcoholism as powerlessness and sickness.

Her guilt is one of her greatest personal problems, and also one of her greatest hindrances in constructive relationship with the alcoholic. She may have a strong need to feel that if she had been different, which may mean "if I had loved him more," he wouldn't have started drinking the way he did; or "if I loved him more now," he would do something about his drinking. To her his drinking frequently means her failure as a woman and a wife. She needs to be helped to understand that alcoholism is powerlessness and that it is because of this, not her, that he is drinking the way he is. When she accepts this and can let the alcoholism be his problem, significant progress has been made. However, it may take time for her to come to the point of really understanding and accepting alcoholism as an illness, and to resolve her sense of guilt and failure. Sometimes she has just as much or more difficulty in accepting the true nature of alcoholism as does her alcoholic husband. Deep within can be the feeling that she "ought to be able to get him to quit drinking."

On the other hand, she may feel that "if he had loved me more," he wouldn't have started his drinking and would surely be doing something about it now. This is why a wife, without understanding, may become hostile over the fact that he is helped in A.A. "He wouldn't let me help him. He wouldn't do it for me. But for them he would." Or she may find it hard to face the fact that she is married to a man who could be and is "licked by alcohol." When such feelings are present they get communicated in one way or another.

For these kinds of feelings, it can be very helpful for her to know that nobody understands why some people become alcoholics, and that alcoholism in one person's life can be simply an expression of a problem common to us all. Information regarding other addictions as well as other forms of defense and escape mechanisms can be helpful.

Hopefully she can be enabled to see that in spite of any problems they have had in their marriage, he is responsible for seeking escape through alcohol. And there is nothing she can do to force him to accept the reality of his condition and seek help. She, too, is powerless over his drinking, but what she can do is establish the kind of relationship with him that will hopefully hasten the day when he will of himself come to such acceptance.

She needs, in addition, to understand the progressive symptoms of alcoholism and come to see them as "symptoms" of the illness. This is difficult because the symptoms are behavioral. It is easy to accept a temperature as a symptom of an infection, or a pain in the side as a symptom of a bad appendix. But to accept his rationalization, alibis, sneaking drinks, grandiose behavior, resentment, and lack of concern and interest in her and the family as symptoms of alcoholism rather than only as signs of "his just not caring" is something else.

Now, how will she use her new-found understanding of alcoholism and the alcoholic in everyday situations? How will it change the relationship she has with her husband?

When she no longer feels guilty, then his resentments and all the rest will not threaten her and cause her in defensiveness to strike back. Rather she will see these as evidences of his own guilt and self-hatred. Imagine the difference when her husband "chews her out" and blames her before or after he has been on a drunk. Now instead of cracking back at him, trying to defend herself, she will say something like this: "If you want to use me as an excuse for drinking, that is okay," or "You really hate yourself after you have been drinking, don't you?" At appropriate times she will share with him her feeling that it looks as if he needs help to overcome his drinking.

Somewhere along the line she will tell him outright that she believes his drinking has gone into alcoholism. This may be a better approach than telling him that he is an alcoholic. She will make clear that she cannot make him do something about his drinking. If he is going to drink he is going to drink, and as long as he continues drinking he will have to accept the results of his drinking, whatever they are. The pain or distress—physical, emotional, spiritual—that most quickly brings the alcoholic to the point of seeking help is that which is built right into the alcoholism itself and which he is allowed to experience fully. When a wife has been helped to the point where she does not try to interfere with his drinking or the consequences of his drinking and really lets it rest with him, then we have a very healthy situation.

What is necessary is understanding and love like that of the father for his prodigal son. How completely he understood and loved! He allowed his son to exercise his "freedom." He didn't try to stop the son in his descent to bondage. He didn't try to seek him out and bring him back. He didn't become overly anxious and fretful about what others would say. He loved him enough to let him go. When the son "came to his senses," what an experience he had upon his return as he realized and experienced the love his father had toward him.

In their new relationship the wife will not be trying to keep her husband from drinking, nor will she be pampering him, covering up for him, moralizing, and pouring hostility upon him. If he can't make it to work on Monday morning, she will not call the boss for him. That problem has developed from his drinking. If he has called her names, "raked her over the coals," etc., when drinking, she will, when he is sober, ask him if he remembers what he said. If he says he doesn't remember, she will recall to him what he said or did, not with hostility, but in the spirit of having it become a part of his awareness while sober. If the creditors start calling, she will, if possible, have them call her husband. The bills are unpaid because of his drinking. If he blames her for bills, she will point out that if it weren't for his drinking, the bills could be met. If his job is in jeopardy, she doesn't plead with his boss but hopes that the boss will bring some wholesome pressures to bear on him to do something about his drinking.

Should he be picked up for drunken driving and put in jail, she will not rush to the pastor or someone else to help get him out. She may ask her pastor or an A.A. person to go see her husband, in order for them to see how he feels about his drinking. Maybe the experience has brought him to realize his need for help. If not, it would be better for him to have to take the consequences as one of the natural results of his drinking.

Any kind of physical abusiveness will not be tolerated. If necessary, she will call the police, have him removed from the house, and/or put in jail. Again his drinking is to blame.

If he wants sexual relations when he is drunk, she will refuse and will talk with him about it when he is sober. She would, if possible, like to have this be a part of their marriage, but it will not be when he is drinking. Such a suggestion may be a little idealistic. Certainly, because of the tensions that have built up and the negative feelings produced by the whole problem, many wives would have difficulty being warm sexually toward their husbands even at times when they are not drinking. Nevertheless, the wife can strive for that kind of attitude.

Whenever possible, the wife can support her husband in his thinking that maybe he does need help and ought to talk with somebody. Leaving A.A. literature around the house may have value even if he gets angry. He may secretly pick it up and read what it has to say. Any knowledge of this sort helps to further spoil his drinking, which is what we want to happen.

The pastor should encourage the wife to tell her husband that she has been in to see the pastor, and to tell him that the pastor would like to talk with him to see "how he feels about it." Quite often the alcoholic will then schedule an appointment. If necessary, the wife should use whatever pressure possible to get her husband to talk with some knowledgeable understanding person.

There may come a time when, if he won't go for help, she will commit him to a state treatment program against his own will. There is a chance that he will come to the point of surrender while there. If not, nothing has been lost. If he comes home angry, she will remember he was angry before she took such action. At least he did have the opportunity, without alcohol in his system, to receive more information about the nature of alcoholism and the help that he needs.

When the wife feels that she is relating constructively to the alcoholic spouse and the problem has reached the point where something must be done because he isn't going for help, many times a very simple reaction works very well. She can make arrangements for him to get into a treatment program. She can tell him what she has done and when a bed becomes available simply say with firmness, "Come on, we are going." Frequently, *if the spouse really means it,* is firm but not hostile, the alcoholic will go.

Often, before legal action should even be considered, a wife may say to the pastor, "I've decided I just can't put up with it any more," indicating that she is thinking of divorce. Usually if she is asked, "Do you think that you are ready and would be able to divorce him?" she gives indication that although she has been thinking about it, she is not yet ready to take such action. As she gains more understanding of the problem, she usually backs away from the idea of immediate divorce and seeks to relate in a more meaningful way to her husband, hoping that this will help lead to his acceptance of his alcoholism.

The day may come when she does seriously threaten him with divorce. She doesn't want to terminate the marriage, but unless he definitely seeks help for his drinking, she has decided to see a lawyer. It is important that she not moralize on this. She should let him know after she has seen the lawyer and when she is going to take specific action. Once she has taken such action, she must stand pat. She hopes that the finalizing of the divorce can be delayed at least a year. This is plenty of time to show whether or not he will accept his alcoholism and seek the help he needs. Before she takes him back, it is necessary for her to talk with a good A.A. member, if her husband has been in A.A., and other experienced people to see if, together with his sobriety, there is real evidence of acceptance and change of attitude. In A.A. it is the question of whether or not he is "really working the program and living their philosophy." Never should she cancel the divorce action on just a promise from him that he won't drink again. If the time for finalizing the divorce comes without any evidence of his being on the road to recovery, she has to decide if she will drop the action and continue to live with him or get the divorce for the sake of herself and the children. The pastor naturally would try to help her in making this difficult and serious decision, but not make it for her.

Early in her efforts to get help, it would be well for her to join an Alanon Family Group. These groups exist for spouses and relatives of alcoholics. They use the Twelve Steps of A.A. for their own problems and seek to help one another in the same manner as alcoholics in A.A. do. Meetings are held once a week. In one of their statements they say that they found, like everyone else, that they were afflicted with pride, self-pity, vanity, and all the things which go to make up the self-centered person; and they were not above selfishness and dishonesty. As their husbands began to apply spiritual principles in their lives, they began to see the desirability of doing so, too. Alanon is available to the wife or husband of an alcoholic before the spouse is in A.A. If there is not a group in the community, a concerned spouse may be instrumental in getting one organized.

If the spouse is unwilling to go to Al-Anon, this raises the question of whether she really believes she needs help for herself and whether or not she may have a need for her husband to keep drinking even though she protests strongly against it. Incidentally, male spouses of alcoholics are welcome at Al-Anon.

Once the alcoholic begins to show interest in getting help, the wife must be careful not to make an issue over it by pushing to make sure "he gets it right now." Although he has often acted like a child and may at times continue to do so, she must not treat him like a child. He needs to make his own decisions as any other adult does. He needs to know that she is expecting him to do something, but to try to force him into action is of no value.

After he is in A.A., there may be a slip or two before A.A. really clicks. Although the wife will initially be fearful, it is important that she try not to communicate her doubts and anxiety to her husband. Nor should she "be walking on tip-toe" for fear that something she may say or do will trigger off another drinking spree. His sobriety is basically his responsibility. The wife needs to be understanding, but she must feel free to be herself without constantly worrying about doing the "right" thing. If he is looking for an excuse to drink, he will find one or make one up. If he doesn't want to drink, he will not use anything the wife says or does as an excuse.

Overconcern about his drinking again may also cause her to try to protect her husband from alcohol. She may insist on avoiding occasions where alcoholic beverages will be served or may want to warn people not to offer him anything to drink. This can only be damaging. If it is his idea, it's a different thing. Usually, however, alcoholics come to feel that they have to learn to live in a world where alcohol exists. They don't seek out places where it is being served, but if they are involved in an occasion where alcohol is included, they feel free and comfortable to say, "No thanks," and drink a non-alcoholic beverage.

In the initial phase of his sobriety, the alcoholic may live and sleep A.A. Consequently, the wife may see even less of him than when he was drinking. This is no cause for alarm unless it continues for a long period of time. It could then be an indication of a "dry drunk," which is just being sober with no real surrender or basic change in attitude.

Real recovery means that he will make amends to his wife for his drinking and all the ways he has hurt her. He will also want to assume his rightful responsibilities as husband and father. Hopefully, the wife will be able to let him do this. Time and effort on the part of both will be necessary to have life get back to some kind of normality. Actually, they may have some very serious problems during his recovery for which they will need help—problems that were present even before alcoholism came into the picture and were intensified by the alcoholism.

All of what has been said is in regard to the so-called normal wife of an alcoholic. There are women who have a pathological need to be married to a drinking alcoholic. Their marriage to the alcoholic is by no means accidental. Should the marriage end in divorce, such a woman may marry another alcoholic after having said, "Never again!" These wives are much more difficult to help. Sometimes, if the husband is going to recover, it will have to be in spite of his wife.

Thelma Whalen, working in a family service agency, observed four types of wives with these pathological needs:

(1) The sufferer who needs to punish herself
(2) The controller who has the need to dominate
(3) The waverer who out of her own pathological need to be loved, appreciated, and given to, searches out the weak and helpless to form relationships with: someone who needs her
(4) The punisher who needs to express hostility on someone else in a controlling situation.[2]

Such a wife will not be able to benefit readily from the counseling already described. No matter how much she is allowed to ventilate her feelings and no matter how much understanding of alcoholism she is given, she continues with the same attitudes and feelings. She isn't interested in help for herself. She only wants to talk about her husband, his drinking and behavior, and her terrible lot in life being married to such a terrible person. Or she may talk about how sorry she feels for him and his great need for her, which is actually her

---

[2] Thelma Whalen, "Wives of Alcoholics," *Quarterly Journal of Studies on Alcohol*, Vol. 14, December 1953, pp. 621-641.

great need for him. Her emotional condition may worsen if the marriage ends in divorce or if her husband recovers.

It is extremely difficult for her to become motivated to look at herself and her own needs. If an attempt is made to have her do this, she often will stop coming in. Sometimes it may prove helpful to ask, "Have you ever wondered if you actually enjoy the situation you are in; that you need to have your husband drinking?" and then directly spell out the particular need that is being met in her life by this marriage. Perhaps even a more direct statement may be of value: "It seems to me, or I get the feeling sometimes, that you actually need to have your husband keep drinking."

The time may come for such a wife, just as for some alcoholics, when it is well to simply point out that there doesn't seem to be anything more to do for her and that it seems she is just going to go on living with the situation the way it is.

If there is an agency or professional person competent and experienced in working with this pathology, certainly an attempt should be made to refer her.

Much has been written and said about such spouses. Frequently the impression is left that this is true of most spouses of alcoholics. Actually the percentage who have a pathological need to be married to a drinking alcoholic may be no higher than 20 per cent.

A word should be said about the children of alcoholics, particularly the older children who can benefit from understanding the sickness concept. Actually some children are hurt emotionally just as much, if not more, by the mother in this crisis as by the alcoholic father. It can be very helpful for them to receive a better understanding of alcoholism. The pastor may feel that it would be good for him to spend some time with some of the children in helping them to understand, rather than to leave it completely with the mother. However, it is better if the mother carries the primary responsibility for this. Alateens, a group of teenagers of alcoholics, is proving to be very helpful. This group functions similarly to the Alanon Group. A pastor may render significant service in assisting the organization of such a group in the community. (In rural areas it may be necessary to have the A.A., Alanon, and Alateen groups include a number of communities.) Sometimes a teenager has been the most effective person in getting the alcoholic to seek help. One alcoholic went for help after his son, with very healthy attitudes regarding alcoholism, simply said to his father, "Dad, you need help for your drinking. We can't help you, but there is help available. When are you going to decide to get some help?"

If the pastor senses that the children have been or are being hurt too seriously in the crisis of alcoholism, he should seek to make referral to a family service agency, if at all possible, so the children can be seen by someone especially trained and experienced to work with them.

In seeking to help, it is vitally important that the pastor function in such a way that his relationship with one is not destroyed in his helping the other. Some counselors say this cannot be done. It is more accurate to say that whenever the counselor is seeing more than one member of a family, there is inherent in the situation the possibility of a real problem. Whether or not it becomes a real problem depends primarily upon the pastor and how he relates with each person in the picture. Experience, hopefully, will show him whether or not he can handle such a relationship.

Primary in consideration of the wife of the alcoholic is the realization that she usually needs as much help personally as does the alcoholic, and that she is often the key person in hastening the day when the alcoholic will quit fighting and accept the reality of his alcoholism.

VII.

ALCOHOL EDUCATION

Alcohol education of some kind is necessary today in the school, the church, and the community. On this point there is general agreement. But on the content and approach of such education there is less agreement.

Attitudes

Attitudes regarding beverage alcohol, its use and non-use, are varied and in some cases heavily loaded with emotion. When we consider alcohol education it is important that we recognize, understand, and accept this variation.

On the one hand, there are those who believe that alcohol is evil, that is, "of the devil." Therefore, Christians should not drink. These people are convinced that this is what the Scriptures say about alcohol and drinking, and thus they interpret passages of Scripture in a way that provides for them the basic foundation of their position. Drinking is usually associated with drunkenness, immorality, divorce, accidents, crime, death, and destruction, and is incompatible with the Christian ethic.

There are others who believe in total abstinence, but indicate that they have a different premise upon which they base their conviction. They don't try to prove from the Bible that alcohol and drinking are evil, even though some of them may personally believe this. Rather, they point to the anaesthetic effects of alcohol, the distorted importance of drinking in our culture, the prevalence of various problems that can be associated with drinking, the large number of alcoholics.

They feel that taking all this into consideration, it is best for the Christian to use his liberty and fulfill his responsibility to his neighbor by abstaining.

Then there are those who believe that beverage alcohol is a gift of God. They do not feel the need to teach people to either drink or abstain. Rather they feel their responsibility is to teach about alcohol, about drinking in our culture as well as other cultures, about abstinence and moderation, about alcohol problems and alcoholism, and then to leave the individual free and responsible to make his or her own decision. Temperance for them can be practiced by abstinence or by moderation.

It would appear that alcohol education would be quite impossible within the church, school, and community, since any group may well contain members who are representatives of these varying attitudes. Yet there is sufficient evidence to indicate that it can be done. There is reason to believe that those who have the first attitude described are today getting a hearing only from members of their own group. Their position is apparently considered "extremist" by most people within our society today. Evidence is present everywhere, however, that people with the other two basic attitudes are coming together in common concern. They are willing and able to listen to each other as well as to work together in efforts to better understand both the nature of the problems and what can be done. They may not agree on whether or not the Christian ethic can apply to both abstinence and drinking. Maybe they will never agree on this, but they realize that such agreement is not necessary before they can be involved in cooperative effort.

Goals

In alcohol education the next basic problem is goals. Attitudes, naturally, have much to do with determining goals. But there is also the question of whether or not the goals in alcohol education are realistic.

For those who believe that people shouldn't drink because alcohol and drinking are evil, the goal is clear: We must teach people not to drink. It is evident that such alcohol education has been effective to some degree in attaining this goal within their own group. However, it is known that many who received such education are drinking today. And certainly this approach has had no significant results in our present society which contains a very high percentage of people who drink. The fact that prohibition through legislation is obviously an impossibility points up that most Americans have not and are not being reached by this kind of alcohol education, either inside or outside the churches.

The modified attitude regarding the total abstinence position has arisen too recently for us to see any indication of its effectiveness in getting people to abstain. Although some of these people may believe that the roots of serious alcohol problems are primarily within the person and not the bottle, all of them would generally accept and promote the idea that people who don't drink can't develop alcohol problems.

Those who believe that alcohol is a gift of God would generally believe that the roots of serious alcohol problems are within the person. They recognize also that a contributing factor is a society in which alcohol has a distorted significance, excessive drinking has widespread social acceptance, and unhealthy reasons for drinking are very much a part of the culture. They would hope that through alcohol education more people would gain a better understanding of alcohol, of drinking in our culture, of the various problems that can exist and develop in the use of beverage alcohol, and through such understanding be better equipped to decide whether they want to drink or abstain. If they did decide to drink they would know what moderation is and what would be the evidences that any serious alcohol problem might be developing in their lives. Hopefully, also, people who would decide to abstain would understand what are healthy over against unhealthy reasons for abstinence.

It can be established that this kind of attitude and approach has been effective in getting people who drink and abstain, and teenagers who haven't yet made a decision, to be interested, open-minded, and reflective regarding the significance and content of alcohol education. There is evidence that this attitude and approach reaches a greater segment of our population.

In any talk about goals, the question is naturally raised as to whether or not alcohol education will prevent people from developing serious drinking problems. We have reason to doubt that this is a realistic goal. Alcohol education can result in greater awareness of and ability to identify the initial indications of personality problems evidencing themselves in the use of alcohol. It also provides a good opportunity for some mental health education in terms of the unmet needs evidenced in the lives of people who use alcohol in unhealthy ways and become problem drinkers or alcoholics. Since such unmet needs are expressed not only in drinking, other problems and addictions with the same basic roots can also be discussed. Attitudes towards alcoholism and alcoholics can be modified. But we cannot expect that alcohol education will change the relationships and/or possible aspects of body chemistry that are the seedbeds of alcoholism.

Certainly there is reason to wonder if all our mental health education has significantly reduced mental illness. However, it has succeeded in changing our attitudes toward mental illness and the care of mentally ill people. In the same way, alcohol education has changed attitudes toward alcoholism and alcoholics and has been effective in providing more treatment facilities for alcoholics. Increasing numbers of people are more readily seeking help. It has also increased awareness as to possible causes and indications of alcoholism. But alcohol education cannot be considered as a major factor in the prevention of alcoholism. In fact, we cannot really talk about or try to accomplish prevention, since no one yet really knows "the cause" or "the causes" of alcoholism.

We know the kinds of problems alcoholics have, but many other people have these same kinds of problems and don't become alcoholics in drinking. As indicated before, alcohol for some people apparently gives some kind of relief or release in a way it doesn't for others and nobody really understands why this is true. Of interest in this regard is the idea, held by some, that certain people are physiologically prone to develop alcoholism if they drink. That there is a physiological factor once addiction is present is evident, but it has not yet been established as a basic cause. Those who believe alcoholism has a physiological origin are seeking to discover what it is. If such an origin is found, it would perhaps be possible by medical examination to determine who can and who shouldn't drink. And there is the possibility that if a physiological factor were found, a medical corrective could be developed that would enable such people to drink without becoming alcoholics.

On the basis of present knowledge and resources, then, alcohol education should be geared at changing, modifying, and possibly supporting attitudes already learned. George Maddox describes such an approach in reference to youth, and his comments can serve as a summary statement of realistic goals for any program of alcohol education: "There is, for example, the task of helping the abstinent youngster to understand his behavior in an environment in which most others are drinking. There is the task of making the youngster who drinks aware that alcohol is not just another social beverage, but an intoxicant which in specific amounts for a given individual has specific effects. There's also the task of helping youngsters to understand the alcoholic as a person with a behavior disorder who can be and ought to be helped. As such understanding increases, the probability of developing attitudes and resources in therapeutic milieu for the alcoholic will also increase. What is needed is not less alcohol education, but alcohol education which is realistically supplemented by a broad concern for identifying and helping the youngster with problems of social and personal development, whether or not his problems are alcohol."[1]

---

[1]George Maddox, "Community Factors in Alcohol Education," *A Report of the Second Conference on Alcohol Education,* held October 16, 17, 18, 1961 at Stowe, Vt.

Content

What should be the content of alcohol education? A good place to start is with the kind of material treated thus far in this chapter, that is, with explanation and discussion of the various attitudes commonly held and the goals we hope to attain. Once such material has been covered, it is important to go over the so-called "facts on alcohol." This information is readily available and we need not reprint it here, but will only mention a few topics as an indication of what should be included.

First of all, alcohol is a food, but a very poor food. It is not a necessary food. Alcohol is also a medicine, but again a poor medicine. Paul's advice to Timothy to take a little wine for his stomach's sake may, in certain instances, be appropriate today, but not necessary because of the existence of other medicines. (Just in passing, Paul's purpose in this suggestion was not to provide a proof text for drinking.) Doctors will on occasion suggest that a person drink moderate amounts of wine, beer, or whiskey, but this in some cases is ill-advised and even risky. It may be the kind of use of alcohol that could eventually lead to alcoholism. Second, alcohol is primarily a sedative, a progressive nervous-system depressant like ether. It affects first the part of the brain which is the center of feelings, judgment, and restraint. Among the millions who drink, a certain percentage will become alcoholics and a much smaller percentage will end up doing permanent physical damage to their bodies. But everyone who drinks is taking into his system a certain amount of anaesthetic. This is the primary and immediate danger in drinking beverage alcohol.

However, alcohol that does not get into the blood is not physiologically in the body. That is, only the alcohol that gets into the blood can function as an anaesthetic upon the brain. Food in the stomach absorbs some of the alcohol, preventing and slowing down the amount that actually gets into the blood. Generally, a couple of mixed drinks or a couple of beers drunk (not gulped) over a reasonable period of time, does not result in over .05% of alcohol in the blood. It is impossible, of course, except under certain control conditions, to predict that a given number of drinks will produce an exact given amount of alcohol in the blood. Besides the factor of food or lack of food in the stomach, other factors enter in, such as the size of the person, the kind of drinks, the amount of alcohol eliminated in the urine, the constant amount oxidized by the body (three-fourths of an ounce per hour), and the length of time in which the drinks are consumed. A person, for instance, who drinks two shots in a hurry is going to end up with a higher blood alcohol level than someone who drinks a couple cocktails in a couple of hours. The proof or the percentage of alcohol of the alcoholic beverage as well as the kind of alcoholic beverage drunk are other factors. With so many variable factors, we need to be careful when we quote "facts" on alcohol in the blood in relationship to the amount of alcoholic beverage drunk.

As the alcohol in the blood increases, the total area of the brain anaesthetized increases. (This is what is meant by the earlier statement that alcohol is a progressive nervous system depressant.) A percentage of .05% (five hundredths of one percent) of alcohol in the blood will have noticeable effect upon the uppermost part of the brain, the frontal lobe. A percentage of .10% affects the motor area so there is poorer coordination and slight staggering. A percentage of .15% is usually considered legal intoxication. (Some feel this should be reduced to .10%.) A percentage of .2% produces excessive staggering, .3% is stupor, .4% is coma, .6-.7% is death. Since it takes about 6-7% blood alcohol to directly harm body tissue, it is obvious that drinking per se is not a factor in this kind of damage. Most physical damage to the drinker is the result of malnutrition that develops from excessive drinking, and not eating an adequate diet.

Except for the fact that a given percentage will produce death, this information on percentages of alcohol in the blood has to be somewhat qualified. Some people can learn to control these noticeable effects and with .3% blood alcohol may not be in a stupor or with .2% may not stagger. On the other hand, some people may act more intoxicated than they actually are. And there are people who are not actually putting on an act, but who at certain times evidence even more intoxication than their blood alcohol level would indicate.

Alcohol education in the church will naturally also include what the Scriptures say and imply about beverage alcohol, drinking, and abstinence.

Wine, which was the common alcoholic beverage in biblical times, is considered a gift of God by the Psalmist. In Psalm 104, "wine to gladden the heart of man" is included among the blessings for which he praises God. In Ecclesiastes 9:7 we read, "Drink your wine with a merry heart." There are many references which make clear that this is a creation of God, the use of which is sanctioned. Our Lord drank wine. He said, "The Son of Man has come eating and drinking. You say, 'Behold a glutton and a drunkard.'" This was not a denial, but rather an evidence of his drinking wine. At the marriage feast, in performing his first miracle, Christ himself sanctioned the use of wine.

The Scriptures also contain some clear, strong condemnations against drinking. Typical of these are the following: Isaiah 5:11-12, "Woe to those who rise early in the morning, that they may run after strong drink, who tarry late into the evening till wine inflames them"; Isaiah 5:22, "Woe to those who are heroes at drinking wine, and valiant men in mixing strong drinks"; Isaiah 28:7, "These also reel with wine and stagger with *strong* drink . . . "; Proverbs 20:1-2, "Wine is a mocker, strong drink a brawler, and whoever is led astray by it is not wise." Proverbs 23:30-32 speaks to those who "tarry long over wine." 1 Corinthians 6:10 lists drunkards together with a group of others who shall not inherit the kingdom of God.

We note, however, that kept within context all of these passages deal not with use but with misuse. The admonitions in Leviticus 10:9 and Numbers 6:3 are limited to special instances and callings. There is strong condemnation of misuse and excess, but nowhere is beverage alcohol branded as "evil" and drinking as "inherently sinful." Actually more scriptural support can be found for moderation than for abstinence if we want to put Scripture to such use. Of course, we do not interpret this to mean that we are to drink in moderation rather than abstain. Beverage alcohol is simply accepted as a gift of God and as the common beverage of the day.

The Scriptures, then, do not answer the question, "Should I or should I not drink?" and in seeking an answer we become involved in considering the moral nature of abstinence and moderation. Abstaining and drinking moderate amounts of beverage alcohol are not virtuous in themselves. Because people can abstain or drink moderately for unhealthy reasons, the key question is, "*Why* do I abstain or drink?" Exploring this question and its possible answers is a vital topic in alcohol education.

The person who abstains because he believes alcohol is "evil" has an unhealthy reason. He is condemning a gift of God and he is also standing in judgment over our Lord, who drank wine. Often inherent in this reason is a "holier than thou" attitude toward people who drink. Any reason that results in such a judgmental attitude is a sinful and unhealthy reason for abstinence.

Abstinence, if it is to be practiced as a Christian virtue, can be seen as a matter of self-denial or as the expression of personal conviction that this is the best exercise, *for me,* of my Christian freedom and responsibility in relationship to my neighbor. The person who holds this conviction comfortably allows other people to make a different decision. For some recovered alcoholics abstinence may be viewed also as a Christian virtue, coming as it may from a type of spiritual recovery. Other sound reasons for abstinence are found in the person who simply doesn't care to drink and in the person who for reasons of health chooses not to drink.

One evidence of the distorted significance that alcohol has in our culture is the uneasiness which people who have good reasons for abstinence often feel when they are offered a drink. They feel the need to say something more than "No thank you." Often they explain that they have no objection if others drink. If we could ever get drinking alcoholic beverages back into proper perspective, these pressures would not exist, either within the person or the group.

Moderation as a means of temperance cannot be defined as simply as abstinence. The word "moderation" is used by different people in different ways. Often it is used to mean only the consumption of moderate amounts. Sometimes, though, it is used interchangeably with the term "social drinking," which for many means acceptable drinking and may include anything, even drunkenness, short of alcoholism.

A proper understanding of moderation involves some understanding of drinking in our particular culture. As one way of getting at this, we can describe, in respect to moderation, five basic reasons why Americans drink. In each case we will consider moderation in terms of morality.

(1) Religious. This is best seen by the use of alcoholic beverage in the Mass of the Roman Catholics, and in Holy Communion of certain Protestant churches. Such use is termed moderate not only because of the amount, but primarily because of the context and reason for the use of the beverage.

(2) Beverage—social. This is moderate drinking like that done and approved in the biblical record. In our day, people who subscribe to this usage drink beverage alcohol sometimes primarily as a beverage and at other times primarily as an alcoholic beverage. It is obvious from the latter use that these people believe it is not inherently sinful to seek a degree of relaxation and well-being in the mild anaesthetic effects of alcohol. Drinking in this case, as in the religious, is properly called moderate because it is moderate in amount, is based on healthy reasons, and exists in the context which sees beverage alcohol as a gift of God.

In this social use, an alcoholic beverage may be drunk before and after a meal. If it is on the table, it will be included in the gifts for which thanks is given to God. Alcoholic beverages may be drunk as a *part* of being together socially. The person who drinks for these reasons has no unhealthy dependence on alcohol and no desire for its violent effects. He does not give alcohol an exaggerated, peculiar sense of importance, and so in a social situation does not pressure others to drink. He will make non-alcoholic beverages available. He will eliminate alcoholic beverages if he thinks it unwise to serve them—they just aren't that important to him. They *are not necessary* for social fellowship. If, in a group of "social drinkers" like this, a non-drinker feels uneasy, it will be because of his own feelings. Members of the group will accept and include him without questioning his abstinence.

Some of these people will on certain occasions, as already indicated, drink to seek a degree of euphoria. This is not an effort to escape the pain of deep-seated anxiety. It is more in the context of having a good time and good fellowship. Exactly what would constitute immoderation in such drinking cannot be specifically defined. Each individual who so uses his personal freedom is likewise personally responsible. Whether or not this kind of drinking falls within the context of moderation is also a personal decision.

(3) Superficial. This word we use to describe the kind of drinking that is termed social drinking by many in our culture. In such drinking, alcohol is given a significance that doesn't belong to this creation of God. It becomes the measuring stick for a person's status, worth, and acceptance as a human being. Common phrases describing this kind of drinking are "smart," the "popular thing to do," "evidence of distinction," "sign of being grown up"; common reasons given for it are "to belong to the group," "to acquire and maintain status," "for business reasons." Drinking, the use of a gift of God, has nothing to do with any of these, and yet in our culture much drinking is done for these reasons. That's why we call it superficial. Those who drink for these reasons exert pressures, expressed or unexpressed, on others to drink. The non-drinker is sometimes even left out.

The individual and members of the group have a low and false estimation of human worth, dignity, and acceptance. In a sense, they are functioning as something less than persons, and revealing a real weakness in their own self-concepts without any awareness of this weakness. Yet many of these people on some level, at some time, feel uneasy and guilty about their drinking without really understanding why.

Even if this type of drinking is moderate in amount, it is immoderate from a moral point of view because of the context in which alcohol exists for these people and the reason they are drinking.

(4) Rebellion. Some people drink to express unresolved hostility toward authority figures in their lives. Among the younger adults who suddenly feel that they have gained new understanding, drinking as an expression of such hostility is sometimes masked under the caption of "Christian liberty." Alcohol drunk even in moderate amounts for such a reason is not truly moderation.

(5) Violent. Here people are primarily drinking for the direct effect of alcohol, either just to get drunk or to relieve tense, anxious, lonely feelings. This kind of drinking is common. Father Ford, a prominent Roman Catholic moral theologian who has made some outstanding contributions in the field of alcohol problems and education, points out the significance of such terms as "beer blast," "slug," "hang one on," "shot." These are violent terms, popular in American drinking vocabulary, which evidence the mood of this kind of drinking and the distorted use of God's gift. Alcohol was not given to man for drunkenness or as an escape from self and reality. Clearly, such use of alcoholic beverage is neither moderate nor moral.

No person can develop alcohol problems as long as his drinking is of the types described under "religious" and "beverage—social." But it is apparent that much drinking in our culture is of the other types, immoderate in context and reason. Certainly the prominence of these types and the acceptance of much of this misuse of alcoholic beverage contribute to the dangers of drinking and the high incidence of alcoholism in the United States. It is, unfortunately, very easy for people in our culture to drink in an unhealthy context, for unhealthy reasons, and without awareness of what all this might eventually mean in terms of serious alcohol problems. It is also possible for people to move from a healthy context into an unhealthy context for drinking.

Because young people can so easily become trapped in the unhealthy situations during the teen years of emotional upheaval and physical maturation, we should pay special attention to alcohol education for teenagers.

Some parents who practice moderation as already defined allow their children to have "little tastes," quite early in life if they so desire. They would hope that the first tasting and drinking be done within the family setting at whatever age they decide is appropriate. Recognizing that attitudes toward beverage alcohol and its use are learned primarily from parents and peer groups, they would like to have the primary learning take place under their guidance.

Many teenagers, however, do their original drinking with their peers. And this frequently is in the "superficial," "rebellious," and "violent" contexts. It is within such a reality that the words of McCarthy, in his book *Teenagers and Alcohol,* are especially helpful: "First, I believe that we must convince young people that the topic and the consumption of alcoholic beverages are sufficiently important so that the individual should not merely drift into the habit, but should make a decision on the matter. Second, I think that the program should be developed in such a way that everything possible is done to persuade each pupil to abstain from drinking alcoholic beverages until he has reached an age when judgment is developed and behavior patterns are established, so that he is capable of making up his own mind whether to drink or not to drink alcoholic beverages. Third, since the decision is an important one, it must be based on facts. Thus, it is necessary to present the facts about the consumption of alcoholic beverages in an unemotional, imbiased manner, and thereby clear up misconceptions and ignorance that exist even today with respect to the effects of the consumption of alcoholic beverages. Fourth, I believe that high school education can and should do much to break down the stigma that exists with respect to the disease of alcoholism and show how the person can be helped and where he can go for help."[2] This latter point applies also to adult alcohol education.

Teenagers should be made aware of why many in their age group drink. If, for instance, in a given situation they can understand that Joe is drinking not because he is grown up, but because by drinking he is trying to handle problems involved in growing up, they can be helped significantly in coping with this sometimes bewildering issue in their lives. They should be presented, too, with the fact that drinking does not resolve the sensitive feelings they have about themselves and in their relationships with other teenagers. There is value in pointing out the possibility that drinking based on such reasons can lead to alcoholism. Of course, most teenagers don't think they are going to become alcoholics if they drink—that's too far away and unrealistic for them. But it can be helpful, attitude-wise, for them to realize that the alcoholic on the road to recovery at 45 years of age has to face, without alcohol, the same feelings and problems he sought to escape through drinking in his teen years.

If the positive approach is used together with good content, teenagers can and will become interested in alcohol education. Within the church it usually will be necessary to have alcohol education as a separate subject for teenagers. At the lower age levels, it is wise to let the education develop naturally as the subject presents itself in biblical stories and teachings.

The matter of "not causing your brother to stumble," of Christian responsibility toward your neighbor in the exercise of Christian liberty, always presents itself in alcohol education within the church.

The simple black and white thinking that is readily used in this regard obviously is neither valid nor adequate. In alcohol education it is paramount that the attitude, content, and method reveal the church's acceptance of the freedom and responsibility of the individual to make a personal decision.

---

[2]Raymond G. McCarthy, *Teenagers and Alcohol,* Publication Division, Yale Center of Alcohol Studies, New Haven, 1956, p. 60.

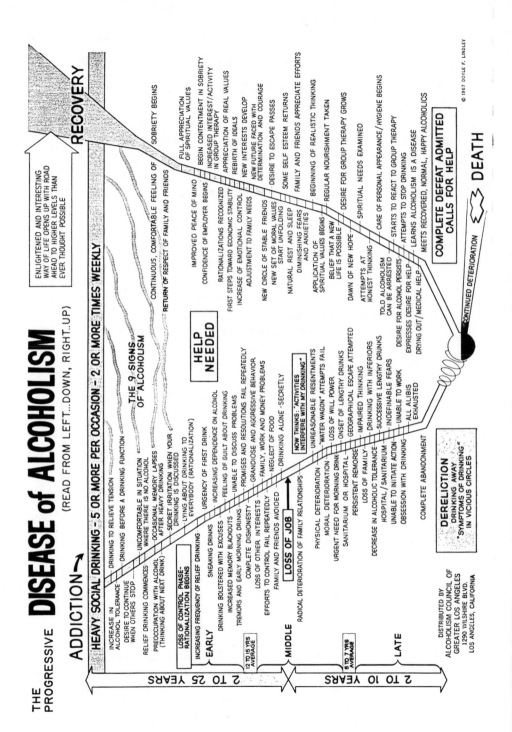

THE PROGRESSIVE **DISEASE of ALCOHOLISM**

(READ FROM LEFT...DOWN, RIGHT..UP)

ADDICTION→

RECOVERY

ENLIGHTENED AND INTERESTING WAY OF LIFE OPENS UP WITH ROAD AHEAD TO HIGHER LEVELS THAN EVER THOUGHT POSSIBLE

HEAVY SOCIAL DRINKING – 5 OR MORE PER OCCASION – 2 OR MORE TIMES WEEKLY

THE 9 SIGNS OF ALCOHOLISM

HELP NEEDED

FULL APPRECIATION OF SPIRITUAL VALUES
BEGIN CONTENTMENT IN SOBRIETY
INCREASED INTEREST / ACTIVITY IN GROUP THERAPY
APPRECIATION OF REAL VALUES
REBIRTH OF IDEALS
NEW INTERESTS DEVELOP
NEW FUTURE FACED WITH DETERMINATION AND COURAGE
DESIRE TO ESCAPE PASSES
SOME SELF ESTEEM RETURNS
FAMILY AND FRIENDS APPRECIATE EFFORTS
BEGINNING OF REALISTIC THINKING
REGULAR NOURISHMENT TAKEN
DESIRE FOR GROUP THERAPY GROWS
SPIRITUAL NEEDS EXAMINED
CARE OF PERSONAL APPEARANCE / HYGIENE BEGINS
STARTS TO REACT TO GROUP THERAPY
ATTEMPTS TO STOP DRINKING
LEARNS ALCOHOLISM IS A DISEASE
MEETS RECOVERED, NORMAL, HAPPY ALCOHOLICS

SOBRIETY BEGINS
CONTINUOUS, COMFORTABLE FEELING OF
RETURN OF RESPECT OF FAMILY AND FRIENDS
IMPROVED PEACE OF MIND
CONFIDENCE OF EMPLOYER BEGINS
RATIONALIZATIONS RECOGNIZED
FIRST STEPS TOWARD ECONOMIC STABILITY
INCREASE OF EMOTIONAL CONTROL
ADJUSTMENT TO FAMILY NEEDS
NEW CIRCLE OF STABLE FRIENDS
NEW SET OF MORAL VALUES START UNFOLDING
NATURAL REST AND SLEEP
DIMINISHING FEARS AND ANXIETIES
APPLICATION OF SPIRITUAL VALUES BEGINS
BELIEF THAT A NEW LIFE IS POSSIBLE
DAWN OF NEW HOPE
ATTEMPTS AT HONEST THINKING
TOLD ALCOHOLISM CAN BE ARRESTED
DESIRE FOR ALCOHOL PERSISTS
EXPRESSES DESIRE FOR HELP
DRYING OUT / MEDICAL HELP

COMPLETE DEFEAT ADMITTED CALLS FOR HELP

CONTINUED DETERIORATION → DEATH

© 1967 DOYLE F. LINDLEY

INCREASE IN ALCOHOL TOLERANCE
DESIRE TO CONTINUE WHEN OTHERS STOP
RELIEF DRINKING COMMENCES
PREOCCUPATION WITH ALCOHOL (THINKING ABOUT NEXT DRINK)
SECRET IRRITATION WHEN YOUR DRINKING IS DISCUSSED

DRINKING TO RELIEVE TENSION
DRINKING BEFORE A DRINKING FUNCTION
UNCOMFORTABLE IN SITUATION WHERE THERE IS NO ALCOHOL
OCCASIONAL MEMORY LAPSES AFTER HEAVY DRINKING

LOSS OF CONTROL PHASE- RATIONALIZATION BEGINS
INCREASING FREQUENCY OF RELIEF DRINKING
SNEAKING DRINKS
DRINKING BOLSTERED WITH EXCUSES
INCREASED MEMORY BLACKOUTS
TREMORS AND EARLY MORNING DRINKS
LOSS OF OTHER INTERESTS
EFFORTS TO CONTROL FAIL REPEATEDLY
FAMILY AND FRIENDS AVOIDED

LYING ABOUT DRINKING TO EVERYBODY (RATIONALIZATION)
URGENCY OF FIRST DRINK
INCREASING DEPENDENCE ON ALCOHOL
FEELING OF GUILT ABOUT DRINKING
UNABLE TO DISCUSS PROBLEMS
PROMISES AND RESOLUTIONS FAIL REPEATEDLY
GRANDIOSE AND AGGRESSIVE BEHAVIOR
FAMILY, WORK AND MONEY PROBLEMS
NEGLECT OF FOOD
DRINKING ALONE -SECRETLY

NOW THINKS: "ACTIVITIES INTERFERE WITH MY DRINKING"

COMPLETE DISHONESTY

LOSS OF JOB

RADICAL DETERIORATION OF FAMILY RELATIONSHIPS
PHYSICAL DETERIORATION
MORAL DETERIORATION
URGENT NEED FOR MORNING DRINK
SANITARIUM OR HOSPITAL
PERSISTENT REMORSE
LOSS OF FAMILY
DECREASE IN ALCOHOLIC TOLERANCE
UNABLE TO INITIATE ACTION
OBSESSION WITH DRINKING
COMPLETE ABANDONMENT

UNREASONABLE RESENTMENTS
"WATER WAGON" ATTEMPTS FAIL
LOSS OF WILL POWER
ONSET OF LENGTHY DRUNKS
GEOGRAPHICAL ESCAPE ATTEMPTED
IMPAIRED THINKING
DRINKING WITH INFERIORS
SUCCESSIVE LENGTHY DRUNKS
INDEFINABLE FEARS
UNABLE TO WORK
HOSPITAL / SANITARIUM
ALL ALIBIS EXHAUSTED

DERELICTION
DRINKING AWAY "SYMPTOMS OF DRINKING" IN VICIOUS CIRCLES

2 TO 25 YEARS

EARLY
12 TO 15 YRS AVERAGE
MIDDLE
5 TO 7 YRS AVERAGE
LATE

2 TO 10 YEARS

DISTRIBUTED BY
ALCOHOLISM COUNCIL OF GREATER LOS ANGELES
1290 WILSHIRE BLVD.
LOS ANGELES, CALIFORNIA

INDEX